D0007324

AN ALLIANCE AT RISK

PUBLISHING FOR THE WORLD
125 Years
THE JOHNS HOPKINS UNIVERSITY PRESS

Laurent Cohen-Tanugi

AN ALLIANCE AT RISK

The United States and Europe
since September 11

Translated by George A. Holoch Jr.

THE JOHNS HOPKINS UNIVERSITY PRESS
BALTIMORE AND LONDON

Originally published as *Les Sentinelles de la liberté:*
L'Europe et l'Amérique au seuil du XXIe siècle,
© Editions Odile Jacob, January 2003

English translation and new preface © 2003
The Johns Hopkins University Press
All rights reserved. Published 2003
Printed in the United States of America on acid-free paper
9 8 7 6 5 4 3 2 1

The Johns Hopkins University Press
2715 North Charles Street
Baltimore, Maryland 21218-4363
www.press.jhu.edu

Library of Congress Cataloging-in-Publication Data

Cohen-Tanugi, Laurent, 1957–
[Sentinelles de la liberté. English]
An alliance at risk : the United States and Europe since
September 11 / Laurent Cohen-Tanugi ; translated by
George A. Holoch, Jr.
p. cm.
Translation of: Les sentinelles de la liberté.
Includes bibliographical references and index.
ISBN 0-8018-7841-1 (hardcover : alk. paper)
1. Europe—Foreign relations—United States.
2. United States—Foreign relations—Europe.
3. Europe—Foreign relations—1989– 4. United
States—Foreign relations—2001– . 5. September 11
Terrorist Attacks, 2001. 6. War on Terrorism, 2001.
7. Europe—Foreign public opinion, American.
8. United States—Foreign public opinion, European.
9. World politics—1995–2005. 10. Islam and politics—
Public opinion. I. Title.
D1065.U5C573 2003
327'.094—DC21   2003010632

A catalog record for this book is available from the
British Library.

For my parents
and
To David and Samuel,
and their fellow citizens of the post—Cold War world,
these basic reference points

Contents

Acknowledgments

This book draws heavily on some twenty years of observation and reflection that led me from a Tocquevillian comparative analysis of the French and American legal and democratic traditions to the political and institutional aspects of European unification and then on to transatlantic relations. Throughout this itinerary I have benefited from the thoughts and experience of a number of prominent intellectual and political figures from France, Europe, and the United States, including Stanley Hoffmann, Robert Badinter, Jacques Delors, Georges Berthoin, Jean-Louis Bourlanges, and many others whom I can only collectively salute.

I also wish to pay homage to Geneviève Seznec, secretary general of the Arthur Sachs Foundation, who for several decades tirelessly searched French academic institutions for talented individuals in all disciplines to send to Harvard University. Like many of my fellow Sachs scholars (as well as Franco-American relations generally), I am indebted to her for her efforts and generosity.

The original French manuscript of this book, like all my previous works, greatly benefited from the comments and suggestions of my brother, Pierre Cohen-Tanugi, and my wife, Jodie, a demanding critic. The American version, which I updated and complemented with a new preface, is principally the joint product of translator George A. Holoch Jr. and copy editor Joanne Allen. Their competence, professionalism, and friendliness made working with them a very pleasant experience. I also wish to thank my

French publisher, Odile Jacob, and her team, as well as the Johns Hopkins University Press team, for their excellent work.

Last but not least, I extend my deep gratitude to my secretary, Patricia Cassini, whose patience and perfectionism were an indispensable part of bringing this project to life.

Preface: The West at a Crossroads

Who needs friends like this? For large sections of American and European public opinion, the diplomatic tensions of the winter of 2002–3 over Iraq have revealed in dramatic terms what is now commonly referred to as the "Atlantic divide."

Although the majority of European governments actually sided with the United States in favor of waging war on Iraq, the widespread feeling, in America even more than in Europe, that considerable damage has been done to the Atlantic partnership can hardly be dismissed. First, France and Germany, two of America's most significant allies since 1945 (and much earlier for the former), went far beyond their own disagreement with U.S. policy toward Iraq to lead an international opposition against it. Second, while national governments were divided, European public opinion made an unusual show of unity against the war (and indirectly against the Bush administration's foreign policy), to an extent that gives credence to the notion of an "ideological divide" between the United States and Europe in regard to international relations, irrespective of official positions. Third, just as the Americans have resented Europe's lack of solidarity over Iraq, the Europeans have resented Washington's patent efforts to divide them, or at least their governments, on the subject. Last but not least, the situation sadly triggered an unprecedented degree of acrimony and bitter rhetoric between historical allies like France and the United States.

This regrettable state of affairs is all the more troublesome because, unlike the tragedy of September 11, 2001, a Euro-American consensus over whether to intervene in Iraq was certainly not the most pertinent test of transatlantic solidarity. The case for military intervention was indeed complex and debatable enough to allow for legitimate differences of opinion about its benefits and risks among longstanding allies. In light of this, the seriousness of the transatlantic clash over Iraq, along with the fact that the French edition of this book was completed just prior to the burst of the Iraqi crisis, strongly suggests that the ills of the Atlantic Alliance, broadly defined, preexisted the Iraqi crisis and will unfortunately survive it.

This book offers an analysis, in historical perspective, of the troubled state of transatlantic relations since the fall of the Berlin wall and of the requirements for their betterment. For a variety of structural reasons, discussed in the first two chapters, since the end of the Cold War the Alliance has become vulnerable, to a degree that governments on both sides of the ocean appear to have underestimated. From that perspective, the failure of transatlantic diplomacy to contain the damage of the Iraqi crisis is largely the result of inattention in both camps to the need to shelter a precious and endangered relationship from the potential divisiveness of post–September 11 geopolitics. The Franco-American crisis over Iraq displayed, on the contrary, the triumph of excess, unilateralism, and separatism on both sides. France went beyond its own legitimate opposition to the war, and America responded to this excess by denying its ally any right to disagree with U.S. foreign policy and military actions.

The transatlantic crisis over Iraq has dramatically reinforced my argument that the principal threat to Atlantic solidarity today is the temptation of each side to view the Alliance as a thing of the past, as if America and Europe no longer shared common values and a common future. For the current neoconservative establishment in Washington, Europe as such has once again proven its irrelevance and its potential nuisance capacity vis-à-vis the United States and therefore the European Union should be treated with benign neglect and its progress toward diplomatic and military integration should be hampered by Washington. Conversely, for at least the

more Europeanist governments, the Iraqi experience is likely to encourage the pursuit of a diplomatic and military capability that is
independent of the United States and designed to serve as a "counterweight" to U.S. supremacy and unilateralism. Longstanding sus-
picions toward one another have thus been strengthened, to the
detriment of mutual trust.

Where does all of this leave us? According to the more pessimistic
view, the crisis of early 2003 inaugurated an era of conflicting interests and sensitivities between the United States and Europe that
will materialize in further differences over such critical issues as the
reconstruction of Iraq, the Israeli-Palestinian conflict, the fight
against terrorism and the proliferation of weapons of mass destruction, and the functioning of the international system generally. In
this context, Europe will remain divided over its relationship with
the United States, and transatlantic relations will essentially fluctu-
ate on a bilateral basis, leaving America's supremacy and unilateralist tendencies unchallenged and its solitude in the world complete.

This book contemplates, and advocates, a more optimistic scenario, one the transatlantic and European crises over Iraq may paradoxically foster. This scenario would stem from the realization on
both sides that the remedy to the present transatlantic rift and the
way out of the longstanding European impasse in matters of foreign policy and defense are deeply intertwined and must be pursued in parallel fashion.

For any sensible observer on either side of the Atlantic the principal lessons of the Iraqi crisis point in that direction. First, transatlantic divisions have had dramatic consequences for the international system as a whole, and Western institutions in particular.
The point hardly needs elaboration in respect of NATO and the
United Nations, but it also applies to European unification, which
has probably suffered even greater damage than transatlantic relations as a result of the Iraqi crisis. The attempt of President Chirac
and Chancellor Schröder to speak in the name of "Europe" in their
active opposition, along with Putin's Russia, to a war in Iraq and to

U.S. efforts to rally the international community to that aim has angered the Atlanticist governments of the Continent and even those smaller countries that have always been wary of Franco-German leadership of the united Europe. In return, the official show of solidarity with Washington by eight European governments, without prior consultation with their fellow member states and with obvious U.S. involvement, was perceived by the founding member states of the European Community as a betrayal of the European spirit. Moreover, "old Europe"'s blunt call to order to the candidate countries of Central and Eastern Europe following their vocal support of Washington legitimately alienated these nations and enhanced concerns regarding the upcoming enlargement of the EU within sections of Western European public opinion. As a result, the traditional dividing lines within the EU—between Atlanticist and Europeanist governments, larger and smaller states, internationally minded and "neutral" nations—have become blurred, undermining not only the prospect of a European foreign-policy and defense capability but the very spirit of European unity and solidarity.

Yet, the second key lesson of the Iraqi crisis is that Europe needs to become at last a responsible and credible player in world affairs and that in order to do so it must develop a common foreign-policy and defense capability. This, however, is unlikely to happen until the EU member states, notably France, Great Britain, and Germany, have agreed on Europe's proper stand toward the United States. The concept of a counterweight to U.S. supremacy appears too ambiguous to be consensual within Europe while the Iraqi crisis has made it unacceptable to American diplomacy. Further elaboration and creativity are thus needed on this critical subject as Europe attempts to heal its internal rift. The definition of a realistic strategic doctrine for Europe in the post–September 11 world would represent a first step in the right direction.

Finally, on the opposite side of the Atlantic, the tensions over Iraq have confirmed that, in policing the planet, the United States would be better off with a stronger, more autonomous Europe on its side, rather than being left alone to face increasingly widespread and virulent hostility from the rest of the world. The alternative--relying on opportunistic "coalitions of the willing," including such reliable allies as Pakistan, Saudi Arabia, Russia, Turkey, or China— should have lost some appeal in Washington after September 11 and the events of early 2003. Similarly, alliances "a la carte" with selected European states against the background of broader European divisions, following the pattern of the Iraqi crisis, would slowly destroy the Atlantic Alliance as well as European unification. In spite of the current temptations in this respect in Washington, this cannot be in the long-term interest of the United States and the West as a whole. Rather, the future lies in a renewed, stable and institutionalized partnership between America and the European Union.

Assuming that these lessons are understood and shared in Europe and America, implementing them will still require a strong political commitment and intelligent leadership on both sides of the Atlantic, along the lines suggested in this book. In the new geopolitical landscape resulting from the end of the Cold War and the attack on the Twin Towers, the Atlantic partnership can no longer be taken for granted, and its preservation will require deliberate efforts and fresh thinking on both sides to cope with differences.[1] The intellectual and political challenge will be to walk the fine line between the denial of a real transatlantic estrangement and the mere acceptance of it without resistance.

If these efforts succeed over the next decade and a new alliance emerges on a mutually reinforcing basis between Americans and Europeans, then Saddam Hussein will have ultimately rendered a worthwhile service to the world, and the vision of President George Bush in his October 1, 1990, address to the United Nations General Assembly may have a chance to materialize: "I see a world building on the emerging new model of European unity, not just Europe but the whole world, whole and free."

June 2003

Preface to the French Edition

This book explores the state of relations between Europe and the United States at the beginning of the new century. Much ink has been spent on the difficulties this relationship has encountered over the last few years, long before the divisions over Iraq revealed them to the world. But the passions that this topic provokes seem to miss the essential point: that a common fate, de facto solidarity, and shared responsibilities unite Europeans and Americans in support of freedom in a world threatened by new forms of totalitarianism.

My own awareness of this deep solidarity dates back a long time. I was born on the shores of the Mediterranean at the time of Tunisia's independence and the foundation of the European Common Market. My childhood was bathed in the light of this cradle of civilizations in which Muslims, Jews, and Christians had lived in harmony for centuries, with the vague sense of forming part of an exceptional community.

Like many other children of my generation, I was marked by my parents' stories about the war, German occupation, Nazi barbarism, and the liberation of North Africa and Western Europe by U.S. troops. France and America have been the two beacons of my imagination, the former embodying language, history, and culture, the latter, enthusiasm, generosity, and security.

Optimism and openness prevailed in the world at the time, through the Atlantic Alliance, the beginnings of European unification, the conquest of space, and the golden age of development assistance, embodied by the International Bank for Reconstruction and Development in the heart of Washington. Learning German as a first foreign language was not only the privilege of good French students, it was almost the expression of a political commitment: faith in Franco-German reconciliation as the foundation of a modernizing Europe fascinated by the "American challenge."

What remains today of this collection of images, which cannot be reduced to the idealized vision of a child of the sixties? The harmonious coexistence of the three great monotheistic religions has practically deserted the shores of the Mediterranean, replaced by the cycle of violence and hatred of the Middle East. The Franco-German partnership has slackened significantly over the years, and along with it the commitment to a political Europe, while the North-South dialogue has dissolved in the great sea of globalization. As for faith in America, it has given way to a more or less virulent hostility from Islamabad to the banks of the Seine.

At least my generation still preserves the memory of the war and the golden age that followed it, and it is capable of contextualizing in the light of history the altered relations between Europe and the United States, France and Germany, East and West, North and South. But what about more recent generations, and what of our children and grandchildren, the generation that came home from school to witness in live broadcast the apocalypse of September 11, 2001, that knows nothing of Jewish-Arab relations but the violence of the Intifada and sees America only through the caricatured prism of the media as a superpower contemptuous of the environment and human rights and inflicting the death penalty on its citizens? What vision of the world can we offer them, and in turn what future are they preparing for us? And how much more deformed and Manichean must be the perspective of millions of children of the developing world, raised in poverty and often resentment?

In the face of this global time bomb, it is up to the political and intellectual elite of each nation to resume the dialogue between civilizations and to fight against the temptation to demonize one another. This task begins here, on both sides of the Atlantic, between

Europeans and Americans, where it is the easiest and, paradoxically, the most necessary, before anything further can be done.

For, against all expectations, the tragedy of September 11 revealed, against a background of worldwide hostility to America, the reality of the divide that has gradually emerged between Europe and the United States. Once the time of compassion, solidarity, and the feeling of shared vulnerability had passed, and despite unstinting cooperation between governments, Europe quickly reestablished its distance from an America entirely absorbed in the war against terrorism. The old irreducible substratum of anti-Americanism was joined by the Europeans' profound misunderstanding of the trauma caused by the annihilation of the Twin Towers and the end of the historical invulnerability of the U.S. national territory, as symbolized by the attack on the Pentagon. The asymmetry in the perception of the threat on the two sides of the Atlantic led first to different analyses of the significance of the event—a state of war on one side, "hyperterrorism" on the other—and then to a growing divergence as to how to confront it—reliance on security and the use of force, if necessary preventive and unilateral, on the part of Washington; emphasis on the political and economic dimensions of terrorism, on diplomacy and multilateralism, in the capitals of Europe. Already present at the time of the Afghan campaign, despite the massive international support for an operation that was unquestionably one of self-defense and public safety, Europe's alienation from the Bush administration has only increased, culminating since the crisis over the appropriate response to the Iraqi situation.

It would nevertheless be mistaken to view the current transatlantic estrangement, as it is often viewed in Europe, in purely circumstantial terms, that is, in relation to the consequences of September 11 and the new tone of American foreign policy. These circumstances were merely the catalyst that revealed deeper changes, the elements of which will come together, if we let it happen, to drive the two poles of Western civilization down sepa-

rate paths. These structural changes account for the recent accumulation of disputes of all kinds at a time when the disorder of the
world should have brought about increased solidarity between
Europe and the United States.

Of course, this solidarity remains in essential areas: governments
and police and intelligence services are actively cooperating in the
fight against terrorism; trade disputes, though widely publicized,
affect only a tiny portion of transatlantic commerce; and the Iraqi
crisis began with successful Franco-American diplomacy in the fall
of 2002, however constrained and equivocal it may have been. Fundamentally, the ties that have united Europe and America for
decades remain much stronger than the propagandists of a transatlantic "ideological divorce" would have us believe. But in a context
marked by the rise of global anti-Americanism and the dramatiza-
tion of every possible difference between Europe and the United
States, peoples are diverging in their thinking, and there are increased misunderstandings between them, fostering reciprocal mis-
trust and preventing constructive dialogue between the two sides
of the Atlantic. Some applaud this state of affairs in the name of the
"emancipation of Europe," even though their latent anti-Americanism is often coupled with an even stronger hostility to European integration.[1] Analyzing the present transatlantic divide in this
way is, however, all the more illusory because Europe is now less
than ever in a position to confront global challenges without the
support of the United States.

The current distance between the New World and the Old is a
source of concern for the preservation of a two-hundred-year-old
relationship and for the future of Europe in a world plagued by
profound disorder. It also raises questions about the stability of the
international system, whose chief guarantor, whether Europeans
like it or not, is the United States. Finally, it is troubling from the
standpoint of the defense and advancement of democratic values,
the common legacy of the two partners of the Atlantic Alliance, as

those values clearly appear not to be universally shared and irreversibly implemented in practice. For all of these reasons the Atlantic divide concerns us all.

Beyond the analysis of the underlying causes of this rift, any attempt at a remedy requires something way beyond the superficial and increasingly bitter criticisms addressed by each of the two protagonists to the other; it requires a Europe assuming fully its responsibilities on the world stage, an America more attentive to the international community, to its sensitivity and its rules, and the restoration of a constructive dialogue between the two poles of Western civilization. May this book modestly contribute to meeting that vast challenge.

December 2002

AN ALLIANCE AT RISK

Chapter 1

THE EMPIRE ON TRIAL

The current estrangement between the two sides of the Atlantic cannot be properly understood outside the context of the tension that developed during the 1990s between the United States and broad sections of the international community. "Why do they hate us so much?" America asked itself in response to the hostile or ambiguous reactions produced around the world by the tragedy of September 11, 2001. The global scope of anti-American feeling was indeed one of the principal revelations of this historic turning point, from the joy of Palestinian children that shocked Western television viewers to the criticisms voiced by readers of *Le Monde* against the solidarity spontaneously expressed by the newspaper's chief editor, Jean-Marie Colombani, in an unexpected editorial[1] and including the ill-concealed satisfaction of many developing nations, official U.S. allies among them, that the Empire had finally been struck at the heart. For Americans, awareness of the sometimes extreme hostility that large segments of humanity felt toward them was a second shock, echoing the September 11 explosions, and perhaps an even deeper one.

The Americans' initial shock was, of course, in response to Islamist terrorism itself and the hostile demonstrations of the "Arab

street." But it soon extended to the rather swift slide on the part
of U.S. allies, including Europeans, from compassion and solidarity to distance, from distance to criticism, and from criticism to antagonism. Far from expressing compassion and sharing in unre-
served condemnation of the barbarism of September 11, millions
of people in the Islamic world more or less openly rejoiced, and
even in the heart of Europe people argued about the event or even
justified it. Since the end of the Cold War there had been talk only
of U.S. "hyperpower," hegemony, and economic, technological,
ideological, and cultural domination, and now a large-scale terrorist operation had succeeded in shattering the myth of invulnerability. It seemed as though the catastrophic collapse of the Twin
Towers had broken a taboo, revealing and further reinforcing an
anti-Americanism of global proportions that had long been fester-
ing beneath the illusions of the 1990s.

From the Americanization of the World to
Global Anti-Americanism

The attacks against New York and Washington did indeed signal
a shift from the decade following the end of the Cold War, which
had been totally dominated by manifestations of American success
and especially by the irresistible Americanization of the world. Ide-
ologically, by the early 1990s the United States had peacefully triumphed after a half-century of armed rivalry with the Soviet
Union. Communism was dead, Eastern and Central Europe had
been liberated, and Francis Fukuyama had proclaimed to the world
the "end of history," meaning the definitive, peaceful, and universal victory of democracy, the rule of law, and the market economy
over every other ideological model.[2] Militarily, the United States
ruled supreme well before the collapse of the Soviet Union, with
no prospect of serious competition anywhere, relentlessly widening the gap even between itself and its European allies, thanks to
its overwhelming technological superiority and vast spending. Its

advanced technology was also the source of unprecedented economic growth: the "new economy," which now appears so distant
in the post–September 11 world, remained a primarily American
phenomenon. Above all, culturally, by widening the scope of their
influence, the Internet and new information and communications
technologies fostered the global dimension of American civilization, the English language, and the American way of life.

   While France, America's only historical rival in its claim to universality, constantly denounced the dangers of hegemony and "hyperpower," the Americanization of the world at work throughout
the 1990s was nonetheless a peaceful process, greeted rather positively by world public opinion. The defeat of communism and the
end of the Cold War was good news for the West, as well as for the
developing world, which too often had been a victim or a proxy in
East-West conflict. The progress of democracy, the rule of law, and
political and economic liberalism[3] in many developing countries as
well as in Europe was rightly celebrated as a significant advance on
the path to world peace. Support for the students in Tienanmen
Square and the fall of the Berlin Wall in 1989, as well as the liberation of the Soviet bloc and of Kuwait two years later, were legitimately credited to the United States. The Clinton administration's
commitment to the values of peace and tolerance, militarily in
Bosnia and Kosovo in support of Muslim populations, diplomatically in the Middle East in the context of the Oslo peace process,
placed American military power at the service of the common
good. The "new economy" fascinated the elites of the world and
opened the prospect of building digital bridges across the North-
South divide. Universities in the United States attracted students
from around the globe, and American popular music and the
American film industry were in the forefront of a world culture increasingly open to diversity.

   This was not all a mirage, and it remains a reality even today.
The breadth of anti-American feeling in the world, a fundamental

fact after September 11, and the reasons for it thus require all the more attention, commensurate with the challenges it poses for peace and the stability of the international system.

Reactions to the new state of affairs established by the Bush administration in response to the September 11 attacks, and indirectly to these events themselves, appear in retrospect as an expression, after a brief interlude for compassion, of the latent antagonism felt toward America by large segments of the international community well before that date. How else can we explain the feelings expressed in some places about the attacks against New York and Washington, from the jubilation of a minority for whom the martyrs of Allah had finally punished the "great Satan" to the more measured hope, more widespread and almost as troubling, that this tragic experience might finally lead America to reform and rediscover the paths of multilateralism and solidarity for the benefit of all? Between these two attitudes, September 11 gave rise to a worldwide debate on the age-old question of the responsibility of the victim for its own misfortunes, ranging from the sense that this was a foreseeable punishment ("He who sows the wind . . .") to the self-scourging of justifying (and relativizing) the annihilation of three thousand human beings in the light of the direct or indirect responsibility of America and the West for all the misery in the world. Al-Qaeda's successful operation thus suspended only temporarily, through the actual, untimely, and of course "unlawful" murder of the accused, the symbolic prosecution that had long been under way against the American empire, from Athens to Göteborg, and from Tehran to Durban, until the desanctification of that empire implicit in the ruins of the World Trade Center encouraged the prosecutors to express their accusations in broad daylight.

This prosecution does not fall under traditional anti-Americanism, a phenomenon of European origin that, as the French scholars Jean-François Revel and Philippe Roger have both shown recently and brilliantly, is ideological, inconsistent, and broadly disconnected from reality or reason.[4] Classic anti-Americanism preceded the founding of the United States and originated in the prejudices of the European (notably French) elites of the eighteenth century toward the New World. It flourished in the nineteenth and twentieth centuries, with the concurrent emergence of America as a democratic capitalist power and of its collectivist countermodel. Anti-Americanism thus had the function, if not the virtue, of bringing together the contrary passions at work in the Old World, those of the nationalistic, authoritarian, and anti-Semitic right on the one hand and those of the anticapitalist, antiliberal, and anticolonialist left on the other.

The contemporary charges leveled against America differ from this historical anti-Americanism insofar as they are not principally European but global, and particularly Islamic, and focus primarily on American foreign policy and its leading role in the spread of "neoliberal," or free-market, globalization. Bright minds point out that such criticism is perfectly legitimate, that it could just as well be directed against any other country and cannot in itself be labeled anti-American. Nonetheless, the numerous connections between this new political and strategic hostility to America and the old underlying European anti-Americanism make the drawing of too strong a contrast between the two unwarranted.[5]

In reality, American foreign policy and the opposition that it generates, notably in the Arab world, along with the question (concerning the West as a whole) of globalization, have long been the principal targets of left-wing anti-Americanism in Europe, expressed in the classic terms of anti-imperialism and antiliberalism. The United States' strategic supremacy, its cultural influence, and its attachment to the security of Israel cause irritation well beyond the left, and the systematic exaggeration of some current transatlantic divergences strongly recalls old anti-American passions. Moreover, hostility to Washington's foreign policy sometimes assumes irrational forms that bring it close to traditional ideological anti-Americanism, when it is not directly inspired by it. In Europe, criticism of George W. Bush's international relations has become a commonplace, a new form of intellectual conformism that leaves room for no argument for or against. More fundamentally, most nations feel ambivalent toward the United States and have contradictory expectations that have every likelihood of being disappointed. America is thus criticized if it intervenes abroad but also if it fails to intervene. Not so long ago Europe scoffed at Jimmy Carter's naïveté and missed Nixon's realpolitik, but it is Carter who has recently received the Nobel Peace Prize, providing an indirect condemnation of the current occupant of the White House. A deus ex machina, Washington has become the scapegoat for all evils and the excuse offered by many nations, European nations included, for failing to take charge of their own affairs. A final notable parallel: the rejection by a part of the Islamic world of modernity, social emancipation, and individual freedom is not that distant from the old French anti-Americanism of the early twentieth century, still slumbering within the confines of the European right.

Once these correlations have been noted, it is important to grasp the specificity of what might be called, as a compromise, global neo-anti-Americanism.

The Price of Power

The new form of hostility to America inaugurated during the second half of the twentieth century was first of all the direct or indirect result of the accession of the United States to the rank of world power, rival of the Soviet Union, after 1945 and then to that of sole superpower after the collapse of communism. The strategic centrality of American foreign policy has thus been the principal element nourishing political anti-Americanism around the world for the last half-century. During the Cold War, the competition between capitalism and communism and Soviet-American rivalry were carried out by proxy in regional or local conflicts in which the United States would side with one protagonist and thereby alienate the adversary. Fluctuating hierarchies of alliances and of contradictory interests, as well as the domestic contingencies affecting

American diplomacy, thus led the United States to trample on its own values by supporting corrupt and dictatorial regimes and to become involved in the domestic politics of many countries, spreading disappointment and resentment in successive waves from Central America, through the Middle East, to southern Asia. The history of Iranian-American or Chilean-American relations over the last half-century illustrates a situation that has recurred in the four corners of the world.

Consistent loyalty to Israel is, of course, the most important aspect of Washington's foreign policy that provokes anti-American feeling around the world, both in the number of nations and populations concerned and in the intensity of the reactions that it provokes, particularly in the Arab and Muslim worlds and in Europe. Even outside Islamic domains this support has become, through the mediation of Soviet, Third World, and anti-Zionist propaganda, the symbol of an alleged neocolonialism hostile to movements of national liberation and to all the wretched of the earth. This unflattering image led to the improbable exclusion of the United States from the U.N. Human Rights Commission in May 2001 and to its condemnation by the pathetic U.N. world conference against racism in Durban, only a few days before the September 11 attacks. The decisive role played by the United States in the Camp David agreements between Israel and the Egypt of Anwar Sadat in 1978 and the U.S. involvement in the Oslo peace process are, of course, omitted by the propagandists who claim that America is anti-Arab and devoted only to the cause of Israel.

Throughout the Cold War, however, American "imperialism" was counterbalanced by its Soviet counterpart, and hostility to the former was neutralized or contained by the misdeeds and danger of the latter. For many Third World countries, America was at the time the bearer of an ideology of combat against Marxism, totalitarianism, and their local variants, accompanied by financial aid and substantial military, economic, and technical assistance. As a power offering protection from Soviet hegemony, it embodied most importantly, in contrast to communism, a prosperous, inventive, and generous civilization. Despite the dark side of the Cold War and the country's diplomatic inconsistencies, in the eyes of Europe and the developing world in the 1950s and 1960s the United States still had the aura of the nation that had triumphed over Nazism and the status of symbol of the free world, spearhead of scientific and technical progress, home of twentieth-century popular culture, laboratory of multiculturalism and civil rights, and cradle of human-rights activism around the world. From Roosevelt to Kennedy, Neil Armstrong to Martin Luther King, Fred Astaire to Humphrey Bogart, and not forgetting Satchmo, Sinatra, and Elvis, the American dream was flourishing, in the far corners of the earth even more than in New York or Detroit.

This positive image began to lose its luster in the Vietnam quagmire. Students and other young people, first in California and New York and then across the country, took up the torch of Wilsonian idealism, stimulating an international protest movement against a political and military establishment that now embodied only force and cynicism. A few years later, in 1974, the Watergate scandal struck another blow against American democracy, whose characteristic moralism and openness greatly magnified an episode that was indeed shameful but would have seemed relatively benign, especially at the time, in many European countries. The crisis within the political leadership of the world's principal power was merely a foretaste of what has since become a common ill of Western democracies. Nixon's realpolitik was followed by the interlude of the Ford presidency and the mixed record of Jimmy Carter, which opened the way for the Reagan revolution, finally victorious over the "evil empire."

Paradoxically, the collapse of the Soviet Union and the end of the rivalry that had been the organizing principle of international relations since 1945 paved the way for a new global anti-Americanism at the outset of the 1990s. For the rest of the world, the end of the communist threat transformed the United States from an ally and protector into a hegemonic power and a policeman, criticized in turn for doing too much and for holding back too often. The "new world order" proclaimed by George Bush following German reunification would never see the light of day. For the North Atlantic Treaty Organization (NATO) and the European Union (EU), the end of the East-West conflict transformed the geopolitical landscape without opening the way to new solidarities and new rules capable in particular of remedying the consequences of the desintegration of the Soviet empire. It also coincided with the Iraqi invasion of Kuwait and the beginning of the Gulf War. For Muslims, the United States was not only the unconditional ally of Israel; it now also embodied the oppressor of the Iraqi people, who were subject to harsh economic sanctions, the military profanation of the holy places of Saudi Arabia (a regime supported by Washington for strategic reasons), and the impiety of a materialistic and decadent society, illustrated by the antics of Bill Clinton. The defense by American forces of Muslim populations against Serbian domination in the Balkans carried little weight against the propaganda that declared the United States an enemy of Islam.

While many nations rejected a presence that they no longer found necessary, the United States showed itself less willing to become involved in world affairs except when its fundamental strategic interests (Kuwait, the Middle East) or human rights in Europe or Africa were at stake. In Iraq and the Balkans local and regional crises have produced at best the formation of international coalitions in which the United States has had the lion's share. Despite its liberation of Kuwait, its contribution to the Israeli-Palestinian peace process, and its humanitarian interventions unrelated to its immediate interests, post–Cold War America became the source of all evil and the focus of all rancor.

"American Globalization"

Perhaps the greatest offense of the America of the 1990s, because it affected the entire world, and Europe in particular, was that it

became the carrier and the symbol of "neoliberal globalization."
The collapse of communism made the market economy the only
term of reference. Ten years earlier, the deregulation process
pushed by Ronald Reagan had imposed an ever narrower vision of
capitalism, elevating shareholder interests over those of other
stakeholders, and strictly financial considerations over industrial,
social, and political aspects of economic life. Before that, the second half of the twentieth century had been marked by the increasing porousness of national economic borders as well as by continuous progress in trade liberalization and expansion. This process
unfolded on a world scale in the framework of the General Agreement on Tariffs and Trade, or GATT, and regionally thanks to the
establishment of the Common Market in Europe and free-trade
organizations in South America and Asia. These regional entities
established ever closer trade relations with one another.

Focused at first on customs duties and industrial products, liberalization gradually extended to agriculture and the services sector, traditionally protected by a thicket of "nontariff barriers."
These regulations, which indissolubly blend protectionist interests
and social and cultural considerations with sometimes ancient
roots, are, even under liberal principles, a matter of legitimate concern for national sovereignty and national identity. The defense
of the "cultural exception," a legal rampart for those concerns invented by the French against the steamroller of globalization, has
thus become an essential dimension of the accusations leveled
against the United States in this area.

Since 1945 the United States has indeed championed the liberalization of world trade, which reflected its political philosophy and
served its long-term economic interests by opening foreign markets to its exports. The misery associated with protectionism during the 1930s provided additional justification for free trade. Washington thus played a major role in setting up GATT in 1947,
supported the establishment of the European Economic Community (EEC) and regional organizations in South America and Asia,

and negotiated free-trade agreements around the world. In the mid-1980s, with the elimination of customs duties generally achieved, it was again the United States that spurred the process of liberalization in the exchange of services, agricultural trade, and rules for international investment in the framework of GATT. This process was a natural extension of the internationalization of national economies that followed the opening of borders, and it reflected the increasing role played by services—telecommunications, intellectual property, banking, insurance, cultural industries, and the like—in the economies of the industrialized countries.

Having pioneered the introduction of competition in these sectors on its own territory through deregulation policies by the late 1970s, the United States felt itself to be in a strong position to conquer foreign markets that would be powerful engines of growth to counter the economic slowdown following the two oil shocks. As a major exporter of services, Europe also should have benefited from the process, except that those sectors were often protected (agriculture, the audiovisual sector), uncompetitive (financial services), or charged with sensitive political and cultural implications (public services, the "cultural exception") and the European Community was not sufficiently organized at the time to meet the American challenge. As for the South, it legitimately felt that it was being offered a fool's bargain, in which it would be forced to open its borders to products and investments from the North while not being in a position to benefit from liberalization.

After years of preparation and difficult negotiations the United States and its trading partners finally concluded the "Uruguay round" of GATT with the signing of the Marrakesh agreements in 1994 creating the World Trade Organization (WTO). But this result was reached at the cost of a transatlantic battle over agriculture and the audiovisual sector, excluded from liberalization in the name of the cultural exception, and with strong pressure on developing countries, for which the price would be paid a few years later in the clash of Seattle. Intended to regulate world trade through law, the

WTO soon became, in the eyes of a heterogeneous coalition of special interests brought together by fierce hostility to America, the very symbol of neoliberal globalization, held responsible for all ills.

In Seattle, Genoa, Porto Alegre, and Florence the antiglobalization activism of the last few years has been only the tip of the iceberg, the worldwide expression of large silent minorities whose social and economic conditions and political reference points have been destabilized by the triumph of a free market without borders that has become associated with the erosion of national identities, industrial dislocation, the weakening of social protections, and unemployment. By the late 1980s European integration had become the principal target of this protest, culminating in France in the emergence of an antiliberal and anti-European movement on the occasion of the September 1992 referendum on the Maastricht treaty. Somewhat paradoxically, the treaty was accused of being both the birth certificate of a technocratic superstate extending to the entire continent and a Trojan Horse for "Anglo-Saxon liberalism." Ten years later the revival of the radical left and the electoral success of the extreme right in France, Austria, Denmark, Italy, and Holland point to the persistence of this antiliberal, nationalistic, and xenophobic current in the social fabric of the Old Continent, a current opposed to European integration and adopting antiglobalist and anti-American positions.

The rise of American power in the course of the last decade could only accentuate the assimilation by large segments of public opinion of the Americanization of the world with the threats of globalization. While the EU was bogged down in its internal contradictions, the United States (whose decline French intellectuals have made it a specialty to proclaim at regular intervals) began a period of unprecedented economic prosperity and ideological, military, technological, and cultural leadership, making it the privileged target of every protest. After Reagan's conservative revolution, ten years of uninterrupted growth combining full employment and low inflation provoked learned debates about the miraculous emergence of a "new economy" of perpetual prosperity. Moreover, neoliberal economic ideas had become widespread in Europe through pension funds, corporate governance, and reliance on the judgment of financial markets and the cult of EBITDA[6] as the ultimate criteria for evaluating corporations, with the consequences that we know in terms of corporate restructurings, job relocations, and, in the end, accounting scandals and industrial and financial disasters on both sides of the Atlantic.

At the same time, this triumphant America, more certain than ever of the universality of its political and economic model, closed in on itself, systematically turning its back on postwar multilateralism. Confronted with international organizations stifled by inefficiency and dominated by a majority of governments hostile to its foreign policy and to Israel, if not to Western democratic values, the United States has, until recently, reduced to a minimum its participation in the U.N. system and its contribution to development policy, increasing a little further the North-South divide and fostering the vicious circle of unilateralism and global neo-anti-Americanism.

Trade liberalization, of course, has been much more beneficial to developing countries than its detractors would have us believe. In particular, it made it possible for the emerging countries in Southeast Asia and Latin America that were able to take advantage of globalization to finally become part of the world economy. But the ideological climate that came out of the 1980s nonetheless helped marginalize the specific question of development, while globalization was simultaneously aggravating inequalities of all kinds. In the 1990s, twenty-five developing countries, with a combined population of 3 billion, experienced per capita growth rates higher than 5 percent per year, that is, two and one-half times the average rate recorded for developed countries. On the other hand, during the same period 2 billion people living in one hundred other developing countries experienced negative growth of about 1 percent.[7] Moreover, integration into the world economy did not spare emerging countries from serious economic and social setbacks during the period, as indicated by the financial crises in Asia, Russia, and Latin America in the second half of the 1990s. Finally, the African conti-nent, the Arab world, and the former Soviet republics of Central Asia have remained at the periphery of the world economy. While the United States was experiencing a period of economic growth un-precedented since 1945, in the course of the 1990s economic growth in Arab countries declined to 0.7 percent, which combined with a demographic explosion to produce massive youth unemployment, a reservoir for radical Islamism. Excluded from modernity and abun-dance, despite the fabulous natural resources of some of them, these countries and their large populations have also remained deprived of democratic development, despite naïve Western proclamations of the joint triumph of the market economy and human rights.

The revelation of global neo-anti-Americanism produced by the September 11 attacks can thus be analyzed as a brutal correction of a monumental error of historical perspective as to the position oc-cupied in the world by the United States and the values it repre-sents at the beginning of the twenty-first century. Already guilty in the eyes of the most moderate Muslims of adopting a double stan-dard in the Israeli-Palestinian conflict, America now appears, in the eyes of huge segments of the world population, to be too power-ful and too arrogant, too prosperous and too egotistical, too influ-ential and too unilateral.

Although they are historical allies of the United States, the Eu-ropeans nevertheless share this feeling too.

Bush the Scapegoat

It may seem surprising to confront the United States with "Eu-rope" as such rather than with the nations it comprises. The abun-dant literature on transatlantic relations, whether dealing with diplomacy and strategy or with sociological analysis, is in fact gen-erally confined to the diversity of national approaches, with the historical Franco-American rivalry and all its contradictions representing the richest and most studied subject. But while there is genuine diversity in European national positions with regard to transatlantic relations, and that diversity remains a substantial obstacle to the emergence of common European foreign and defense policies, the construction of Europe has now reached a degree of maturity such that most areas of contention between Europeans and Americans no longer have much to do with national particularities or prerogatives but rather give rise to a convergent, if not unified, attitude on the part of the majority of Europeans. This observation is encouraging because it demonstrates that Europe is finally beginning to exist as an entity and as an autonomous political personality distinct from its member states. But it is also cause for concern because the emerging European identity tends to assert itself in almost structural opposition to the United States, in a perhaps deeper way than Franco-American rivalry, which has been tempered by historical ties and real affinities between the two peoples.

With the exception of a few discordant voices, stupor, compassion, and solidarity were expressed throughout Europe on September 11, 2001, and in the following weeks. But while official cooperation never wavered, this state of grace did not last in public opinion, and the prosecution of America returned to the fore, in the media and among the elite, with surprising rapidity. Such a reversal, or rather the persistence of criticism despite the enormity of the event, probably stems first of all from a difference in perception as to the significance of September 11. The Americans were struck in their heart, on their protected territory, and in the very symbols of their power. Although the citizens of Europe were also threatened by Bin Laden and his troops as Westerners and "Judeo-Christians," and even more vulnerable, they viewed the attacks from a distance, sometimes disputed their character as acts of war, and essentially saw them (sometimes with absolute good faith) as fallout, however frightful, from American foreign policy in the

Middle East, Iraq, and Central Asia, with Washington's negotiations with the Taliban on strategic interests and oil quickly coming
to the fore, just as the motive of oil has been overwhelmingly put
forward in the debate over Iraq. September 11 was thus seen mainly
as an American affair, calling for genuine concern from Europe but
also sometimes evoking the satisfaction of the weak upon witness-
ing what they deemed the proper punishment of an arrogant protector and powerful rival. One had to be a dedicated supporter of
America, paranoid, or endowed with an acute strategic sense to
share with the other side of the Atlantic the feeling of a historic
turning point, a declaration of war on Western civilization, if not
on all humanity. The European voices that spoke out in the months
that followed, calling on public opinion to take a true measure of
the event, generally met this description. It was wasted effort, however: the persistent misunderstanding by many Europeans of what
remains a total trauma for American has played no small role in the
current transatlantic estrangement.

The second explanation for the ephemeral character of European solidarity has to do with the swiftly disappointed hope that
the September 11 ordeal would finally bring America to reform
after years of egotism and unilateralism, that it would lead America
back to the righteous path of multilateralism and openness to the
rest of the planet, in particular to Europe and the developing
world. Encouraged by the clever effort of American diplomacy to
build a global coalition against terrorism, this hope, legitimate at
bottom but rather perverse in the circumstances, vanished with the
preparations for the Afghan campaign. It then became clear that
the United States expected from the international community only
political support for a military operation that it intended to conduct alone, with interference from no one, including NATO. Subsequently, the overthrow of the Taliban regime and the destabilization of Al-Qaeda in Afghanistan, the success of antiterrorist
diplomacy, and control of the American domestic situation thanks
to the calm patriotism of the population have restored America's

self-confidence, while confirming its feeling that in hard times it could count only on itself.

America thus came out of the ordeal of September 11 morally and politically strengthened, and more unilateralist than ever. Somewhat vexed, the Europeans contributed to this outcome by their inability to assume their portion of the military burden in the antiterrorist battle, but even more by their relative insensitivity to the import of the event for the United States as well as for the international system as a whole. The Americans, for their part, cannot understand how Europe, so prosperous and in the process of unification, can fail to assume its international responsibilities and to affirm more clearly its solidarity with a nation to which it owes so much.

From that point on, with one misunderstanding leading to another, the vicious circle of mutual criticism and resentment between Europe and the United States was restored. Unilateralism consists in defining one's conduct in relation to one's own vision and one's own interests alone, which of course presupposes the ability to provide for one's own needs. This attitude is encouraged and fostered by the certainty of being able to count only on one's own strength. Anti-Americanism, for its part, like all deliberate ill will, always focuses on the negative, systematically minimizing the positive aspects of U.S. actions or the justifications for them and just as systematically denouncing their defects, deliberately exaggerated by the media. Thus the psychological gap created by September 11 between the two sides of the Atlantic could not help but strengthen America's determination to respond as it chose, alone if need be, to the terrorist threat.

In this general context Europe's criticism of U.S. foreign policy found a convenient scapegoat in George W. Bush. Rather than declaring hostility to the United States, much less to the American people, the enemies of the "Empire" went after poor W., the questionably elected president, fresh from his native Texas, simplistic and belligerent in temperament and surrounded by a coalition of hawks, oilmen, and fundamentalists prepared to drag America,

Europe, and the world to the edge of the abyss. Europe was not suffering from anti-Americanism, but from an allergy to the personality and the politics of Bill Clinton's successor and his neoconservative entourage, as evidenced on the president's first European tour, in July 2001, and any spread of the infection to the American people as a whole was thus only the result of the support granted by a traumatized nation to its dangerous president. It is true that the majority of Europeans had not "voted" for Bush and that the new Republican administration had inaugurated its mandate by a series of unilateral reversals that had caused turmoil in Europe: intent to disengage from the Balkans, repudiation of several international treaties, relaunching of the antimissile program.

The problem is that this comfortable distinction between a likeable America and a disastrous president is not seriously defensible, for at least two reasons. The first is that most of the alleged symbols of the Bush administration's unilateralism are merely the extension of positions taken by the Clinton administration, such as the latter's reserved attitude (to say the least) toward the treaty establishing the International Criminal Court, as well as toward the Kyoto Protocol on the reduction of greenhouse gases, which was overwhelmingly rejected by the Senate in 1999. These positions in reality reflected, as we shall see later, permanent aspects of U.S. diplomacy with respect both to the economy and to America's attitude toward international organizations. The second and principal reason is that the continuing popularity of this president, whose election was indeed questionable, expresses a very deep political reality that his European critics do their utmost to ignore: the leadership demonstrated by George W. Bush in the conduct of the country's foreign and domestic affairs following September 11, in extraordinarily difficult circumstances, and the nearly unanimous acceptance by American public opinion of the necessity of waging a relentless war against terrorism. The unexpected Republican victory in the November 2002 elections, more than a year after the attacks, confirmed the solidity of that support.

One may be a fierce partisan of the Democrats, have no liking for the blunt style of George W. Bush, wish that Al Gore had defeated him, and prefer the charisma of Bill Clinton, but it would be intellectually dishonest to deny that very soon after September 11 Bush was able to meet the challenges he faced and to find the right tone in addressing his people and the rest of the world, including the Arab and Muslim communities. One must also recognize that Secretary of State Colin Powell demonstrated remarkable talent in cementing the antiterrorist coalition and preventing things from getting out of hand in Pakistan or elsewhere in a highly risky situation. Finally, one must acknowledge that the Afghan campaign, in which many hastily foresaw another Vietnam, made possible in record time and with extraordinary efficiency the overthrow of the Taliban regime and the destabilization of Al-Qaeda's local infrastructure.

Far from matching the caricature of the simplistic and warlike Texan decried by so many Europeans, George W. Bush quite simply put America back on its feet; not only that, and this is often forgotten, his determination considerably reduced the terrorist pressure that was weighing on Europe in the wake of September 11. Ironically, it was this new American contribution to European security that fostered the swift resurgence of anti-Americanism among Europeans, even if it was clothed in simple hostility to a man and his policies. Briefly baffled by the speed of the U.S. military victory in Afghanistan—what would we have heard if America had gotten bogged down?—the Empire's prosecutors swiftly turned their criticism against its aftereffects: the conditions in which the Guantanamo prisoners were held, the president's State of the Union speech on the "axis of evil," rearmament and the evolution of American strategic doctrine, continued pressure on the Iraqi military arsenal, and, no doubt with greater legitimacy, America's diplomatic absence from the Middle East.

Style and tone may change, but it is clear that the war against terrorism and its consequences will persist after George W. Bush has gone and will make up the principal axis of American foreign policy in the medium term. In these circumstances, what significance can be attributed to the resurgence of "political" anti-Americanism in European public opinion? Is it nothing but the return, excessively publicized in some countries, including France, of the old left-wing anti-imperialism, refurbished with the fantasies and resentments provoked by globalization and by the assertion of American power against "terror"? Or is the harm more widespread, more complex and deeper, and therefore more problematic for the future of transatlantic relations and of the community of values on which they are based?

Chapter 2

CONTINENTAL DRIFT

Neither simple recurrence of age-old anti-Americanism nor passing antipathy to a president and his foreign policy, to which the United States would merely react by treating Europe with indifference or contempt, the gulf that has now developed between the two sides of the Atlantic unquestionably represents a deep trend. The result of a series of developments at work on both sides of the Atlantic and on the international stage, it is reflected in an accumulation of differences of all kinds, as though the relationship between Europe and America had now become one of structural conflict.

Heavy Weather over the Atlantic

Despite being comparably publicized, these differences are not all equally important barometers of transatlantic relations. The first area of contention between Europe and America, the oldest and the most natural considering the competitive relation between the two principal world economic powers, concerns the application of international trade rules and the persistence of more or less disguised protectionist measures, notably in sensitive or strategic sectors such as steel, agriculture, and aeronautics. These questions are handled pursuant to the dispute-resolution mechanism of the

World Trade Organization. The European Union has exclusive jurisdiction in this domain to defend the economic and trade interests of its member states and makes good use of it against the
United States. Although they are widely publicized, these disputes
affect less than 5 percent of transatlantic trade and are generally resolved by a mixture of legal guerrilla warfare, economic pressure,
and political negotiation.

Because of the recent broadening of the agenda of multilateral
negotiations, supported notably by Europe, these classic trade disputes now extend into debates related to the environment, public
health, social standards, and, more generally, the regulation of the
world economy. This extension means that the two mastodons of
world trade now not only argue on concrete interests, such as ba-
nanas and steel, but are also placed in contention, in front of the rest
of the world, on questions of political and economic philosophy of
global concern, ranging from genetically modified organisms to the
access of developing countries to drugs to the control of greenhouse gas emissions. America's rejection of the Kyoto Protocol on
the reduction of greenhouse gas emissions in particular caused considerable turmoil in Europe and the rest of the international community in light of the global risks related to climatic change and
the responsibilities of the world's principal polluter in this area.
Each of these issues involves considerable political, financial, industrial, and commercial stakes, with respect to which both Europe
and the United States legitimately defend their interests.

The areas of foreign and security policy form another, much
more important level of transatlantic divergence. In the diplomatic
realm the disagreement is nothing new, having to do particularly
with attitudes toward the Israeli-Palestinian conflict, with the Europeans seeing America as too favorable toward Israel, and vice
versa. The defeat of the Oslo peace process sponsored by Bill Clinton and George W. Bush's lack of engagement against the cycle of
violence arising from the second Intifada have strongly revived criticism in this area from Europe and the rest of the world. More gen-

erally, the Europeans have reservations about the central role attributed to the fight against terrorism in the new American foreign policy, and even more about the almost exclusive emphasis placed on the use of force and the politics of security in this domain. The recent transatlantic confrontation on the Iraqi question is particularly telling in this regard. In this context the blessing given by the Bush administration to the Sharon government's fight against Palestinian terrorism has given rise to a twofold misunderstanding in a Europe traditionally favorable toward the Palestinian position.

On strategic issues the new situation following September 11 has strongly increased divergences, now having less to do with the evaluation of the threat than with the manner of dealing with it. The American plan for an antimissile shield, made concrete by the abrogation of the 1972 Soviet-American ABM treaty, and changes in American doctrine on the use of force—the notorious "preemptive war"—deeply worry the Europeans, as does the explosion of the American military budget. On each of these issues the unilateralism of the decision intensifies the questioning about its import and its implications for collective security and transatlantic relations.

A third area of tension, more recent but far from anodyne, has to do with philosophical, ethical, and social questions and generally with "values," a subject on which Europe has grown increasingly critical toward the United States. Regular use of capital punishment in several American states, the treatment of prisoners at Guantanamo Bay from the perspective of human rights and international conventions, the sway of religion, moralism, and political correctness over American political life and society, the most inegalitarian aspects of the American social model, and the tendency toward the commercialization of all things are in various degrees shocking to European sensitivities.

Finally, at the intersection of foreign policy and ideology, the negative attitude recently manifested by the United States toward the construction of an international order based on multilateral institutions and the rule of law has alienated large segments of the

European public. The distance established since the Reagan years
from the U.N. system, and particularly the systematic and
undiplomatic rejection by the Bush administration of several international treaties of worldwide concern—the Kyoto Protocol,
the treaty instituting the International Criminal Court, and treaties
banning antipersonnel mines and small-arms trade—illustrate in
European eyes America's repudiation of postwar legalistic multilateralism in favor of an egotistical and unilateralist approach to international life whereby realpolitik expresses lack of solidarity with
the community of nations. Rarely exposed to public opinion, the
arguments invoked by the United States to justify its positions
carry little weight against the widely publicized image of an
America attached to its consumption of energy and to the freedom
to purchase firearms and hostile to international criminal justice.
And American isolation from an international community feder-
ated by Europe on these highly symbolic issues only increases bilateral tension.

The ambivalence and rivalry have, of course, never been absent from
Euro-American relations; in the midst of the Cold War Henry
Kissinger spoke of transatlantic "misunderstandings," and Franco-
American differences have been emblematic for two centuries.
Similarly, European anti-Americanism was manifest before the end
of the Cold War, the rise of globalization, or the events of September 11. Indeed, criticism of American foreign policy has been
an identifying characteristic of the left-wing European intelligentsia at least since 1945, with the French leading the way. Nevertheless, transatlantic solidarity never failed at critical moments
and on essential matters, even under de Gaulle, for example, during the 1962 Cuban missile crisis. The issue then becomes whether
the developments observable on both sides of the Atlantic over the
last fifteen years are likely to alter that historical reality over the
longer term, regardless of official positions.

The question is far from academic. The last decade has wit-
nessed a series of deep transformations in the international order

that came out of the postwar period: with the end of the Soviet Union, the disappearance of the common threat that had weighed on both sides of the Atlantic and thereby assured solidarity; the re-unification of Germany and the Old Continent, coupled with the increasing affirmation, if only at the level of aspiration, of the European Union as a political actor on the world stage; and finally, and paradoxically in light of the foregoing, the evident "uncoupling" of the two partners to the Alliance, in social and economic matters as well as on military and strategic ones. To benefit from the proper historical perspective, an analysis of the impact of these transformations on the future of transatlantic relations must extend from the postwar heritage, which gave rise to the Atlantic relationship in its current format, to the tendencies at work since the collapse of the Soviet Union and, even more radically, since the dividing line of September 11, 2001.

The Golden Age

Even within the youngest generations, most Europeans still know that they are indebted to America for their salvation twice in the course of the first half of the twentieth century, thanks to its decisive intervention in the two world wars and the liberation of Europe from Nazi barbarism. They also know that thanks to the Marshall Plan (representing the equivalent of 100 billion euros from 1948 to 1951, that is, 1.5 percent of the American GDP at the time), the United States contributed substantially to the economic reconstruction of a continent that had been devastated by years of warfare and suicidal nationalism and protectionism, that it provided military protection throughout the Cold War, and finally that it contributed significantly to the emancipation of Central and Eastern Europe from Soviet domination. But fewer young Europeans, perhaps, are aware that the United States also supported the birth and development of European unification itself in the form in which we know it today.[1]

Even before America's entry into the war the Roosevelt admin-

istration had carefully studied the plans for a federal organization
of the European continent sketched during the preceding decades
and then within the French Resistance. The objective of the United
States, which had once again been compelled to get involved in a
world conflict of European origin, was already to "prepare the
peace" by integrating the destructive nationalisms of the Old
World into a political organization larger than the nation-state. It
was also necessary to resolve the question of German power while
avoiding the tragic diplomatic mistake committed by the Allies at
the end of the First World War of humiliating defeated Germany
in the Versailles treaty. This interest in the unification of the continent developed by 1945 into active support and gave rise up to
the early 1960s to extraordinary cooperation between Americans and
Europeans under presidents Truman, Eisenhower, and Kennedy.

The Europeans were represented by Jean Monnet, who, before
becoming the founding father of Europe, was a high-flying lob-
byist and a peerless diplomat. Having been a banker in the United
States between the wars, Monnet had excellent connections among
the elite of the East Coast, who were then a small and influential
community in major universities, business circles, the legal profes-
sion, and the administration, and in think tanks such as the Council on Foreign Relations, where all these worlds came together.
This golden age of transatlantic relations was in fact characterized
by an ease of movement and relations between government, university, financial, industrial, and philanthropic circles and by the
resulting cooperation between the public and private spheres. It
should also be credited to a generation imbued with the idea of
public service and an internationalist vision of the future. It was
with this line of American visionaries—John Foster Dulles, Dean
Acheson, John McCloy, George Kennan, George Ball, Averell
Harriman, and McGeorge Bundy, mostly members of the State
Department, but also open to parallel and informal diplomacy—
that Jean Monnet and his Action Committee for the United States
of Europe were to carry out the political reconstruction of the con-

tinent over the course of the fifteen years following Allied victory over Nazi Germany.

From Washington's perspective, the idea of European unification provided an arena for the expression of enlightened self-interest. The first priority was to ensure political stability and economic reconstruction in Europe, necessary for prosperity and for the survival of Western democratic values, in keeping with the lesson that the American political elite had drawn from the First World War: any domination of Europe by a totalitarian power of any variety would undermine those values even on American soil. Moreover, despite interwar protectionism, in the late 1940s Europe remained the United States' largest export market, so that the economic collapse threatening Europe immediately after the war could not leave America indifferent.

For these two reasons, European unification in a federal and democratic form presented several advantages in the eyes of the internationalist visionaries of the time. First of all, it made possible a solution to the problem of German power, while placing German economic resources at the service of reconstruction in a way that was politically acceptable on both sides of the Rhine. But European unification also made it possible to defuse destructive nationalism, including in the area of trade, in order to foster a peaceful, open, and market-oriented economic entity.

This first series of considerations was soon joined by the ideological and strategic challenges of the East-West confrontation. Immediately after the war, the Truman administration had briefly considered the possibility of including the Soviet Union in the process of European unification. The "coup" of Prague in 1948 and the beginnings of the Cold War soon eliminated such speculations: American diplomacy became resigned to the at least temporary division of Europe and of Germany. From then on, the economic and political unification of Western Europe, along with the Atlantic Alliance, was naturally seen as a powerful means of strengthening the Western camp against the threat of Soviet domination. The success of the operation would, moreover, serve as a permanent magnet for the "people's democracies" of the East, helping in the long run to bring those countries into the Western orbit and leading to the reunification of the continent.

The only remaining uncertainty was the role Great Britain intended to play in the process, which it was hoped would be a leading one. The early rejection by the British government of any European organization producing a loss of sovereignty led the Truman administration to support Monnet's proposal for unification based on Franco-German reconciliation, embodied in the 1950 Schuman Plan for a European Coal and Steel Community (ECSC). Soviet advances in the East and French preventions against a tandem with Germany without British participation led the United States to provide military protection to Western Europe in the form of the North Atlantic Treaty, which established NATO in April 1949.

The foundations of the European and Atlantic order of the Cold War were thus set, and successive American administrations provided cooperation and active support to the various stages of European unification throughout the 1950s, from the ECSC through Euratom and the European Free Trade Association (EFTA) to the EEC. Fifty years later one can only be struck by the openness and visionary intelligence of postwar American diplomacy and by the nearly total success that history has so far granted it. The bets made by the enlightened advisers of Roosevelt, Truman, Eisenhower, and Kennedy produced the effects that they anticipated, from the British joining the Common Market to the gradual erosion of Soviet domination of Eastern and Central Europe, opening the way to the reunification of the continent through the extension of the European Union to the east, something the United States had always favored.

But this golden age of European-American relations now seems to belong to a distant past.

The Time of "Misunderstandings"

This fortunate era began to fade from the very beginning of the Johnson administration, gradually giving way to more complex and strained relations between the two sides of the Atlantic. The changing of the guard in Washington, the disappearance of the postwar generation of internationalists, obviously provides a preliminary explanation for the change in climate, given the decisive role played by a handful of men with close ties who were committed to the common and almost sacred cause of the invention of a democratic European and Atlantic order. The second, decisive factor had to do with structural changes at work on both sides of the Atlantic.

The United States was then increasingly absorbed by the Cold War, from the Cuban crisis to the Vietnam War, which had a long-lasting effect on America's domestic politics and identity as well as on its external image and foreign policy. Europe, for its part, was out of the woods. By the early 1960s American economic aid, the opening of borders in the framework of the EEC and GATT, and national measures of modernization and reform had borne fruit, opening a long era of prosperity that came to an end only with the repercussions of the first oil shock in 1973. The EEC was now established as a commercial rival of the United States, and the two parties confronted each other through more or less hidden subsidies and protectionist measures to increase their access to each other's markets, as well as to those of the rest of the world, in both declining industries (steel, textiles, automobiles, agriculture) and high-tech and other promising sectors (aeronautics, defense, cultural industries).

In the diplomatic and military field, the establishment of the iron curtain in Europe had displaced the Cold War onto other continents, where America was already alone in assuming the defense of the "free world." But France under de Gaulle, not satisfied with having blocked British entry to the Common Market in 1963, challenged American domination in NATO and withdrew from its

integrated military command in 1966. This challenge was continued in the aspiration, essentially rhetorical at the time, to establish an independent defense capability intended to become the
"European pillar" of NATO. The United States was already criti-
cizing the Europeans for not assuming their fair share of the burden of their own defense, while the Europeans (or some of them)
accused the Americans of intending to monopolize all aspects of
the strategic command of the Alliance. Not surprisingly, the dispute cut through the ranks of Europeans, whom it still divides into
"Atlanticists" on one side and "Europeanists" on the other. The
former, under the aegis of Great Britain, were content with American military protection and were prepared to pay the political price
for it. For Great Britain, as for Holland, Portugal, or Denmark, the
defense of the European continent had to be based exclusively on
NATO under American leadership. The latter, led by France, de-
manded European participation in the strategic command of the
Alliance and agitated for a "European" Europe, that is, independent from the United States. In de Gaulle's view, that Europe was
intergovernmental, and its defense was based primarily on cooperation among national military forces, in a balanced partnership
with the United States. Like London, Paris had secured nuclear
weapons in order to count in the game of deterrence that characterized the Cold War. Sharing a similar tradition of national sovereignty, independence, and universalist diplomacy, the two capitals thus embodied contrasting visions of European-American
relations. As for Germany, France's privileged partner in the early
decades of European unification, its heavy historical burden excluded it from defense questions for a long time. Divisions among
Europeans, coupled with internal contradictions in French positions (between national sovereignty and Europeanism) and American positions (between burden sharing and a monopoly over decision making), in a relatively frozen strategic situation, ensured the
absence of a European defense capability and the reign of NATO
under American command through the eighties.

Finally, the opportunities created by the perverse effects of Soviet-American rivalry, notably in the developing world, led Europe,
or at least those countries that were not Atlanticists, to attempt to
embody a "third way" between the two superpowers or even between capitalism and communism. Beginning in the mid-1960s,
industrial competition, trade disputes, and diplomatic battles about
European foreign and defense policy thus became mandatory and
increasingly frequent patterns in transatlantic relations, particularly
prominent at the time in French-American relations.

The Europeanists of the State Department, who had begun
working with Jean Monnet toward the unification of the Continent
in 1945, had of course anticipated the economic and trade competition that a united Europe, made more efficient by its conversion
to the market economy and free trade, would inevitably enter into
against the United States. But they had rightly considered that that
was the price that had to be paid for the construction of an economically and politically stable democratic entity that could be a
substantial strategic ally as well as an economic rival of the United
States. Similarly, they had wanted to leave it to the Europeans to
organize their unification on their own terms and had foreseen that
once Europe had become a political reality, it would necessarily
emancipate itself from American positions, creating the risk of opposition between the two sides of the Atlantic. This possibility as
well had appeared to be a necessary evil, and those who feared it
the most had anticipated either that the plan would not be fully re-
alized or that in any event an independent but democratic and liberal Europe would never be very far from American positions on
essential matters.

These expectations turned out to be correct throughout the Cold
War and remain largely so today, out of ideological solidarity to be
sure but also because the European Union is still not an international political player independent from the United States, notably
on the essential question of its security. It is nonetheless true that
for the last ten years rivalry, antagonism, mutual ignorance, and

unilateralism have taken precedence over the deep complicity and solidarity that had dominated transatlantic relations since the end of the war in spite of diplomatic and trade crises. The question thus arises, posed by Messrs. Kissinger, Brzezinski, and other major figures of American diplomacy, whether future progress toward European emancipation will not end up eroding transatlantic ties and weakening their historically decisive contribution to the stability of the international order and the promotion of Western democratic values.

America and the European Identity

Two major changes in the geopolitical context that occurred simultaneously at the beginning of the 1990s intensified this concern. The first effect of the disappearance of the Soviet military threat against Western Europe and the developing world was the destabilization of all the institutions constituting the postwar international order, including European unification itself, which had been fostered by that threat. The European Community avoided existential vertigo only thanks to the political advances promised by the Maastricht treaty, ratified by a narrow margin in 1992. The weakening of transatlantic ties that had begun with the fall of the Berlin wall thus was part of a larger challenge to postwar Western institutions as a whole, beginning with NATO, which is now open to its former enemies to the East. This destabilization of frameworks and ways of thinking established in the context of the confrontation between East and West relegated to the background the traditional transatlantic dispute over a European autonomous defense capability. Once the common enemy had disappeared, the United States began to demand that Europe assume responsibility for the conflicts linked to the implosion of Soviet domination over the continent. At the same time, the wars in Bosnia and Kosovo demonstrated the Europeans' inability to restore peace on their immediate periphery without substantial American military participation.

Paradoxically, the second decisive change involved the gradual transformation of the EEC into a political union intended to play a role on the world stage. This transformation, which took place amidst conflicts between "federalists" (or integrationists) and "sovereignists" (or nationalists) inside each European country, forced those countries to ask themselves some painful questions that the pragmatism of the Monnet method, based on the establishment of practical solidarities giving rise to ever closer ties between peoples and nations, had spared them up to that point. How was European political identity to be defined? What were the purposes of the EU? What should its geographical borders be, and what position should it assume in the new international environment? How should globalization, which was transforming the societies of Europe and operating as a lever for the opponents of European integration, be dealt with?

Answering such questions, which European leaders have never liked to address and for which they have done nothing to prepare public opinion, has been made even more difficult by the continuing enlargement of the Union, which will soon include ten new Eastern and Central European nations. In addition to the effect of numbers, the integration of countries historically neutral or lacking in universalist ambitions, of former communist dictatorships, of a series of small countries created by the disintegration of larger entities, and eventually of the Muslim nation of Turkey, even though it has a secular constitution, will significantly confuse reference points for identity, borders, international positioning, and purpose within the European Union. In the face of these existential difficulties, and thanks to the pacification of its geopolitical area, the political Europe in formation has naturally tended to find a common answer to these ontological and strategic questions in an increasingly systematic differentiation from the United States.

On the question of identity, the attempt to define and the emphasis placed on the "European social model," the "cultural exception," a multilateralist political sensitivity acquired in the experimentation involved in European integration itself, and, more generally, all the possible factors establishing an ideological distance from the "American model" fulfill a twofold function: to bring together an ever larger and more disparate group of nations that the Soviet threat no longer unites, on the one hand; and to legitimize European unification itself for public opinion through a convenient distinction from "American globalization," on the other. The formulation of the European Charter of Fundamental Rights and the notion of Europe as a shield against globalization are a part of this process, which is objectively fostered by American unilateralism and the emphasis on American exceptionalism. This politics of identity tends to project an essentially pejorative image of the United States, fed by old or new European stereotypes of an America that is violent, inegalitarian, racist, bigoted, uncultured, archaic, and unilateralist, symbolized precisely by the death penalty and incarnated by the Texan George W. Bush.

In addition to this twofold internal benefit, differentiation from the United States also provides a response in the realm of the purposes and the external positioning of the European Union. It enables Europe to assert itself on the international stage as a mediator between American unilateralism and the diversity of the world, as the standard-bearer of a humanized and regulated globalization, as a force balancing American power, midway between North and South. The approach is not fundamentally novel: it fits into a natural continuation of nonaligned diplomacy and the "third way" between the two superpowers, favored by Gaullist France during the Cold War in order to increase the influence of France and Europe in the world. Similarly, the concern with a differentiation in identity also takes its place in a largely French tradition of preservation of national particularities in the face of "Anglo-Saxon liberalism."

The changed circumstances since the Cold War period are nonetheless doubly significant. For Europe, it is no longer a matter of refusing to choose between two superpowers engaged in proxy conflicts, but of distinguishing oneself from the only superpower, who happens to be its ally and historical protector. Further, it is no longer the mid-sized power nostalgic for its grandeur that was Gaullist France but an economic body and a political union in formation consisting of several hundred million citizens that is adopting this position on the world stage. We can relativize this difference by recalling that European unification has always been ontologically defined with reference to the United States, that it aimed at giving birth, through the "United States of Europe," to a second democratic center necessarily distinct from and in competition with the first but one that would be its alter ego, and that a balanced dialogue with America still remains one of the principal and legitimate reasons for its existence. It nonetheless remains the case that in the existential quest that the European Union is confronting, systematic differentiation from, or indeed opposition to, the United States has tended to become a formative and fundamental dimension of its identity and of its diplomacy, which seems very distant from the initial vision of Jean Monnet and his heirs.

This attitude, moreover, largely transcends the split between left and right and the opposition between federalists and sovereignists. It prospers as much among the activists for European unification, traditionally liberal and internationalist, if not pro-American, as among nationalists of both right and left, for whom anti-Americanism is second nature. A recent attempt at defining European political identity, emanating from a most reputable source, named as values specific to EU secularism, "which distinguishes us from both the United States and Islam," "attachment to a social market economy, in which solidarity serves as a principle for the organization of the economy and of society," and finally "a conception of international relations that establishes a legally organized framework and a form of multilateral cooperation that the United States has increasingly rejected. We should also note that there is a growing distance between the code of specifically European values and that of the Americans."[2] The United States is explicitly designated twice and implicitly targeted by the second criterion.

Paradoxical at a time of globalization, the opening of borders, and mass tourism, the ideological and cultural distance characterizing the development of American and European societies is quite real. Of course, it is exaggerated to some extent by the current tendency of the Europeans to systematically assert their difference from the United States in the realm of "values" and on a whole series of social questions, such as the death penalty, abortion, human rights, and the relations between church and state or between men and women. The fact remains, however, that American society is increasingly shaped by issues and attitudes that are foreign to European sensitivities, like political correctness and the rigidity that it imposes on social and individual relations or the widespread invasion of bureaucracy and litigation. Increased mutual understanding fostered by increased contact, therefore, intensifies awareness of differences more than it helps to reduce them, all the more because the mobile elites of globalization operate in a professional and technical world that is as narrow as it is homogeneous, a world in which attempts to deepen political and cultural dialogue get short shrift.

The development of the economic, human, and consequently political geography of the United States in the course of the last twenty years has also contributed to the current distance in European-American relations. The economic and technological boom of the last two decades has propelled Texas and California, and more generally the South and the West of the country, to the rank of centers in competition with the Northeast, Europe's historical point of entry into the New World. This displacement of the centers of economic and demographic growth in turn brought about a shift in political personnel and sent to Washington men of the West (Reagan) and the South (Bush) who were unfamiliar with Europe and with Atlantic culture. Reagan's conservative revolution, moreover, inaugurated an era of decentralization in which power was broadly shifted from Washington to the states. These tendencies were joined by a certain deterioration of American politics, which has European equivalents, linked to more rapid turnover in elected federal officials and to the domination of money, the media, and communications professionals over the functioning of democracy. The result has been an increasing provincialism in political personnel and political debate, tending to distance Washington from Europe, if not from the rest of America.

The technological and economic gap that has developed between the two sides of the Atlantic has also contributed to this continental drift. During the period from 1991 to 2000 the United States experienced an exceptionally long phase of economic growth coupled with minimal inflation, increasing productivity, and near full employment. The revolution in information and communications technology, which was partly responsible for this growth, showed American advance in those sectors, which are strategically important for the future. And that advance is partly responsible, along with the intensity of competition in the economy, for the gap in productivity between the United States and Europe recorded since the mid-1990s. According to an October 2002 study by the McKinsey Global Institute, since the mid-nineties France and Germany have stopped catching up with American productivity as they had been continually since the postwar period. According to McKinsey, this "uncoupling" is generally tied to Europe's inability to reduce and adapt regulatory burdens on business that function as brakes on competition. In addition, there is an increasing gap in research: according to the European Commission, American research investment exceeded that in Europe by more than 100 billion euros in 2000, and the gap had doubled over the preceding five years. Private investment in research and development in Europe is estimated to be half that in the United States, again because of penalizing regulations in areas such as biotechnology and genetic research, as well as because of lesser efficiency in public expenditure. The less favorable environment for research in Europe also explains the deficit in human capital: 5.1 researchers for every thousand employed people compared with 7.4 in the United States.

As political speeches about the knowledge economy and innova-
tion proliferate at the European level, it is easy to imagine the
repercussions of these handicaps on future growth, productivity,
and employment on the Old Continent.

But it is the spectacular contrast between demographic trends
on both sides of the Atlantic that will have the most important effect on the relative positions of the two partners of the Alliance in
the coming decades.[3] Whereas the Europeans are still experiencing demographic decline tied to the continuous decrease in fertility
rates since 1945 (the rate has now reached 1.4, well below the 2.1 required for stability), since the 1980s the United States has reversed
the trend, so that its rate is approaching 2.0. The conjunction of a
higher fertility rate, notably in the rapidly growing Hispanic population, with large-scale immigration has produced unanticipated
growth in the American population, which should exceed that of
Western Europe between 2030 and 2040 and should reach half a
billion in 2050, compared with 280 million in 2000. During the
same period, it is likely that the population of Western Europe will
decline from its current level. The United States would thereby become the only major industrialized country to experience a demographic growth rate comparable to those of the major nations of
the South. In 2050 the median age would thus remain stable at
about 36, while in Western Europe it would move from the current 37.7 to 52.7, and those over 65 would represent the equivalent
of 60 percent of the population of employment age. If these projections materialize, the Old Continent would never have so well
deserved its name. The economic implications of this demographic
contrast are obvious: Beyond the effect of numbers, making the
United States the largest solvent consumer market in the world,
America would benefit from an ever younger, active, dynamic, and
multicultural population. Europe, on the other hand, would suffer from an impoverishment and a demographic aging that would
put a strain on its growth and its public finances and would rein-
force its conservatism and its nations' resistance to change.

Sociologically, because of massive immigration since the 1950s, American identity now has come to fully include Hispanic, Asian, Afro-American, and even "multiracial" components and has made the promotion of diversity the alpha and omega of social relations.[4] According to demographic projections, the non-Hispanic white population, that is, of European origin, will no longer be a majority in 2050. In foreign policy these developments are strengthening the interest that the United States has always had in Latin America, Asia (particularly China), and the former Soviet bloc. In contrast, the European Union is now seen as a pacified and unproblematic area that remains a difficult and uncertain ally because of the complexity of its institutional structure and the ambivalence of its diplomatic positions. The United States generally criticizes the EU for devoting considerable energy to attempting to resolve its internal contradictions, to the detriment of the contribution it could make to resolving the major problems of the world in partnership with the United States. In response to the caricature by which it is represented in Europe, America happily replies with the image of a conservative Europe, preoccupied above all with social security and the reduction of the work week, morally exposed to criticism, and constantly threatened by a return of its old demons. The new context arising from September 11 provoked worry in the face of the resurgence of extremism, anti-Americanism, and anti-Semitism in several European countries, including France.[5] The gap between ways of thinking is fostered by the emergence of globalization and international terrorism as central issues in contemporary international relations, in which Europe could find itself just as easily playing a complementary role as being in ideological conflict with the United States. A final element, and not the least important, is that the demographic contrast between the two sides of the Atlantic is very likely to perpetuate, and even to increase, the already huge gap between the U.S. and European military budgets, with major strategic consequences.

The Great Split

The concern over a strategic "uncoupling" of the United States and Europe, that is, divergent or even antagonistic developments on either side of the Atlantic, is as old among the most Atlanticist of Europeans as the creation of NATO itself. But that fear was traditionally linked to Gaullist efforts to distinguish European foreign and defense policies from those of Washington. The ghost of a transatlantic uncoupling is now in the process of becoming a reality, but this is more because the United States is jettisoning Europe as irrelevant than the converse.

This situation is the result of a slow process, begun well before September 11, 2001, but the attacks on New York and Washington greatly accelerated and clarified it. This process has three aspects: a decreasing place for Europe in the strategic priorities of the United States, an unprecedented gap between European and American military capabilities, and, since the fall of 2001, a unilateral redefinition by Washington of world geopolitics and the appropriate strategic doctrine to deal with it.

From 1949 on, relations between Europe and America were founded on NATO, a political and military alliance serving as a pillar of American foreign policy with respect to the Soviet Union. The end of the Cold War initiated the disengagement of American forces from Europe and opened a period of uncertainty, during which the nature and the missions of NATO lost clarity and specificity, before recovering a short-lived second wind in the Balkans. This parenthesis was closed with the lightning strike of September 11, 2001. The strategic priorities of American diplomacy and defense policy were thereafter directed toward the fight against international terrorism, now embodying the principal threat to collective security. For Washington, the principal theaters of the war against terrorism are located in Central and Southeast Asia, the Middle East, Africa, and the United States itself rather than in Europe, where the situation seems to be under control for the moment.

Having thus lost its status as the principal prize in the confrontation between East and West and the privileged ally of the United States, Europe does not have much to offer the Americans for the defense of its own territory, much less in the struggle against the new global threats. For American strategists, the transatlantic gap in military capabilities has become so great that, except for British special forces and some French assistance, the European contribution amounts to practically nothing, and it may even be negative because of operational incompatibilities and the lack of weapons coordination. The result has been, after the revealing experience of the Kosovo war, a peculiar division of labor: the Americans "do the cooking," leaving it to the Europeans to "help old ladies cross the street in Pristina," or less crudely, the Europeans take care of peacekeeping and finance nation building, in the Balkans as in Afghanistan, after the Americans, alone or with local help, have taken care of making war. This division of labor may be found offensive in Europe, but one must recognize that the American analysis is not without basis and that the transatlantic gap in military capabilities will only grow larger.

The U.S. defense budget for 2001 already amounted to more than twice that of the fifteen members of the European Union ($310 billion, or 2.8 percent of GDP, as opposed to $144 billion, or 1.4 percent of GDP), while the effectiveness of European military expenditure is less than that of the United States because of the lack of coordination among various national programs and weapons systems. The all-out rearmament decided by the Bush administration in the wake of September 11 was expected to raise that budget to $379 billion in 2003, an increase of $69 billion in two years, much higher than the total French and German military budgets, and an increase of at least $160 billion has been programmed for the next ten years. According to experts, since October 1, 2002, the United

States has spent more than $1 billion a day on defense. In contrast, the three major European nations—Great Britain, France, and Germany—substantially reduced their defense budgets and their military research and weapons expenditures in the course of the 1990s. In France the budget was reduced to 1.8 percent of GDP in 2000 (compared with 3 percent in the 1980s), and in Germany it fell to 1 percent. Despite all the rhetoric about European security and defense policy, neither the member states taken individually (except for the United Kingdom and, to a lesser extent and recently, France) nor *a fortiori* the European Union itself has proposed a rearmament program capable of initiating a real attempt to catch up with the United States.[6]

Besides, Europe is handicapped by the budgetary situation of its member states and by the constraints of its stability pact, whereas the Bush administration has so far been able to take advantage of the large surpluses accumulated in the Clinton years. Europe will be even further harmed by the massive budgetary charges imposed by the dramatic aging of its population in the next few decades. In these circumstances, the qualitative and technological gap between military forces on the two sides of the Atlantic is in danger of becoming irreversible, compromising the ability of the Allies to intervene effectively together. As in the past, American rearmament will have beneficial consequences for American research and the American defense industry, in which mergers have accelerated in recent years, to the detriment of more or less successful efforts for consolidation in this sector in Europe.

Finally, its military supremacy has enabled the United States to transform in a few years, if not a few months, the strategic doctrine in force since the Cold War on the basis of its analysis of the new dangers threatening international security and, particularly since September 11, its own territory and its citizens around the world.[7] These new threats are defined by their ubiquity, their multifarious character, their enormous dangerousness, and their freedom from any moral, legal, or governmental constraint, as well as from any political rationality, however radical. They can strike any target in any location, from distant theaters to the metropolises of Europe and America, with any weapon, including nuclear, chemical, and biological ones, using international networks and technologies rooted in the modern West, abolishing the boundaries between national defense and international order, between internal and external security, between terrorist networks and terrorist states, between ethnic conflict and war against the West, and defying the categories of the law of nations and the most basic humanity. These threats are joined, of course, by "traditional" border or ethnic conflicts like the Gulf War and Kosovo, which are unlikely to disappear and call for ever more sophisticated conventional weapons.

In the face of these new threats, opposite from those of the Cold War, security can be thought of only in global terms, and the doctrine of the use of force has to be developed in a fundamentally different way from what prevailed in the age of nuclear deterrence and the subsequent era of negotiated disarmament and Soviet-American détente. The "balance of terror" has been replaced by the asymmetry of mass terrorism. The United States, therefore, secured Russian agreement in 2002 to the abrogation of the 1972 ABM treaty, which had ended the arms race, in order to pursue the program for an antimissile defense shield of American and allied territory, designed to intercept in space missiles from terrorist states or organizations. In addition, and even more controversially, the United States has enlarged its doctrine on the use of force in order to include the prevention of future threats. Once a terrorist organization or a "rogue state" has attempted to acquire weapons of mass destruction and declared its intention of using them unilaterally against the United States or its allies, the logic of deterrence becomes inoperative because it presupposes rules based on relations between states and especially, for the potential attacker, on the fear of reprisals. These two elements are obviously lacking in the kamikaze hyperterrorism inaugurated on September 11, 2001.

Finally, according to the *Nuclear Posture Review*, addressed to

Congress by the Pentagon in December 2001, the United States now intends to include some nuclear weapons among preventive measures against the nuclear, chemical, and biological arsenals of openly hostile powers (North Korea, Iraq, Iran, Syria, Libya) or even in response to aggression initiated by one of those countries against the United States or its allies. This doctrinal change is said to have been coupled, in violation of the nonproliferation treaty, with the development of new nuclear weapons of low or variable yield, able in particular to reach deeply buried sites from which weapons of mass destruction might be launched. The resumption of American nuclear tests, under a moratorium since 1992, is also included in the plan. Presented as a mere adaptation of deterrence to the multifarious nature of new threats, the new American nuclear military doctrine has finally closed the book on the Cold War, deepening the operational and philosophical gulf that now separates Europe from America on strategic issues. While there may be a consensus in the international community on the nature of the threat, ideas about its intensity and especially about methods and strategies for dealing with it are increasingly divergent on either side of the Atlantic. Militarily weak, Europe tends, naïvely or not, to make multilateralism, diplomacy, and development aid, that is, political and economic treatment of the problem at the root, a panacea, whereas the American superpower is convinced of the necessity of nipping in the bud, militarily, unilaterally, and preventively if necessary, the major danger represented by international terrorism in all its forms, including state forms, wherever it may be harbored.

In the new global geopolitics outlined by the Clinton administration as early as the mid-1990s, the reunified Europe and NATO enlarged to include its former communist adversaries were marginalized both as strategic states and as participants in the process of decision making and implementation of the war against terrorism. According to the Pentagon, the nature of any particular mission in the context of that war determines the shape of the appro-

priate coalition to carry it out, and not the converse, as during the
Cold War, when everything was articulated around the sacrosanct
missions of the Alliance. Residual disputes over the command of
NATO and the autonomy of European defense policy seem laugh-
able now that the American elder brother has in a sense said
farewell to a Europe out of its depth.

In this new geopolitical landscape, and in the face of this strategic revolution carried out at breakneck speed by the United States,
what future remains for transatlantic solidarity?

Chapter 3

THE NEW ATLANTIC IMPERATIVE

Investigating the resilience of the essential bond that has united Europe and the United States since the Enlightenment transcends the narrow, recurring issue of the fate of NATO in the post–Cold War world. It calls for much deeper questioning about the stakes and about the conditions of the preservation of strong transatlantic relations in the new global geopolitical environment and in the face of the centrifugal forces just analyzed.

The Day When Everything Became Possible

In the early 1990s, in the euphoria of the end of the Cold War, solidarity between Europe and America seemed less critical. At the time, Francis Fukuyama's thesis of the "end of history" celebrated, to considerable acclaim, the worldwide triumph of liberal democracy and the market economy over communism, as well as the end of any serious ideological confrontation between the West and the rest of the world.[1] Once the West had extended everywhere and no longer faced any major adversary, transatlantic relations lost any real specificity, and they could now just as well be characterized by rivalry as by solidarity.

But this optimistic vision was short-lived, thoroughly demol-
ished by the barbarism that soon followed the fall of the Berlin
wall, even on European soil. Conflict and "ethnic cleansing" in the
former Yugoslavia, the resurgence of neocommunist and neofascist
movements in Central and Eastern Europe, the rise of religious
fundamentalism and political extremism, the Rwandan genocide,
and the proliferation of "failed " and "rogue" states—the end of
communism engendered a vacuum and chaos rather than a new international order. All of this undermined Fukuyama's argument, or
at least its popularized version, although it did not constitute a sufficiently serious threat to the liberal Western order to provide a
new raison d'être for transatlantic ties.

The threat became concrete on September 11, 2001. It was
known that the disintegration of the Soviet empire had fostered the
formation of international terrorist networks and the proliferation
of weapons of mass destruction that could be used against civilian
populations by nonstate actors outside the framework of an offi-
cially declared war. The hypothesis had, however, never material-
ized and thus remained in the nature of a risk. The attacks on New
York and Washington represented its concrete verification, not
only confirming the possession by hostile forces of global organi-
zational capacities and means of mass destruction but especially revealing the determination of educated men who were integrated
into modern society to use them. The transgression of the moral
prohibition against destroying one's own life and the lives of a large
body of the civilian population, which until then had served as an
implicit barrier to the capacity for harm, was without question the
most overwhelming aspect of the attacks on the World Trade Center and the Pentagon for anyone who still retained any illusions
about human nature. September 11 was the day when everything
became possible, first and above all because a moral barrier had
fallen and also because it inaugurated the unnatural alliance between the most nihilistic political and religious intolerance and the

most formidable strategic and technological effectiveness. The
United States' ability to organize a large coalition against terrorism, the subsequent redefinition of international relations, and the
diffuse but widespread feeling that we had entered a new era with
troubling prospects clearly resulted from the revelation of the
henceforth unlimited nature of the threat. The discoveries made
since then about the extent and the resources of Al-Qaeda, a truly
global network, have strengthened that feeling.

One might have thought that an event of this kind, extraordinary both in itself and because of its many repercussions, would
suffice to rejuvenate the Atlantic relationship in the name of solidarity and due to the community of interests and values that has
united the two centers of Western civilization for two centuries. In
fact, when the planes captured by Al-Qaeda crashed into the Twin
Towers and the Pentagon, and Europe and America anxiously took
the measure of their vulnerability in the following days and weeks,
the thesis of the "clash of civilizations" developed by another distinguished American scholar, Samuel Huntington, seemed to have
triumphed over that of his former student Fukuyama.[2] Often caricatured without having been read, Huntington takes the opposite
view from that of the end of history: in his eyes the post–Cold War
world, far from reflecting the universality of the Western liberal
order, is characterized by a multiplicity of both power centers and
civilizations. The bipolar world of the colonial era and of the East-
West conflict has been replaced by a plurality of centers of power
that tend increasingly to correspond to the major civilizations.
Contrary to the illusions inherited from the nineteenth century, the
modernization at work in many cultures, notably in Asia and the
Middle East, has not been a synonym of Westernization, much less
of the emergence of a universal civilization. On the contrary, it has
been absorbed and shaped by local and regional paradigms, when
it has not exacerbated them in various forms of fundamentalism
and other affirmations of identity. The emerging cultural antagonisms at all geopolitical levels have been accompanied by the rela-

tive long-term decline of the West in the face of the rising economic and political power of Asia, the demographic explosion of
the Muslim world, and the growing and increasingly virulent political and cultural affirmation of the civilizations of the East against
the values, the institutions, and the liberal democracy promoted by
Western civilization. From these historical and geographical analyses emerges a grid for understanding the post–Cold War international order, structured around conflicts of civilizations rather than
by economic or ideological competition. The end of the East-West
conflict, which had structured international relations for a half-century, had fostered the illusion of a general pacification of the planet
even though the collapse of the Soviet Union was precipitated by
Moscow's defeat in Afghanistan at the end of the first modern confrontation between Muslims and Westerners and as the Gulf War
was about to break out.

Still, although tragically illustrated in its conflictual dimension
by the attacks on New York and Washington, as well as by Bin
Laden's media dramaturgy, the thesis of a clash of civilizations
caused fear and soon became a foil for antiterrorist diplomacy. No,
September 11 was not the first act in the war between civilizations
predicted by Huntington, the first act in the millenarian revenge
of Islam against the Judeo-Christian West; believing that would be
playing the game of radical Islamism and would provoke precisely
what we are seeking to avoid. In fact, one of the principal weak-
nesses of Huntington's argument is that it ignores the contradictions and antagonisms at work within each civilization, and particularly within Islam. It is thus necessary to dissociate Islam and
Islamism and to see in the jihad only a rhetorical weapon used by
terrorists for essentially political purposes against America, Israel,
and moderate and Westernized Arab regimes.

The seriousness of the September 11 attacks has, moreover,
compelled the international community to reevaluate terrorism
and nearly unanimously condemn it, even if the United States
alone has the means and the political will to wage real war against

it everywhere. Applying the label "terrorist" to movements calling themselves movements of national liberation and using terror
against an adversary who was by definition more powerful had for
decades been a matter of controversy in the United Nations and
elsewhere, with Arab and other developing countries always dis-
puting that characterization of the Palestinian resistance against Israel, whatever weapons it may have used. September 11 overturned
that situation by transforming both the means and the ends of terrorism and consequently the relationship between them. With respect to means, hyperterrorism and the risk of the proliferation of
weapons of mass destruction in the hands of international networks, but also of uncontrollable states, have changed the dimensions of the threat and weakened the traditional alibi of the in-
evitable resort to terror by the weak against the strong. Similarly,
the noble causes that in the eyes of some justified this kind of violence have given way to nihilism or, at the very least, to a radical
hostility to the values of any civilization in the name of a fanaticism
increasingly removed from the political objectives usually pursued
by such movements. Finally, the conjunction of the inhumanity of
the means and the obscurity of the ends has made Islamist terrorism a radical threat to the peace and security of the world, thereby
discrediting the resort to terror in all its forms.

Like the excessive optimism of the end of history, the pessimism
of the clash of civilizations in its vulgarized and bellicose form has
also been rejected, all the more firmly because Islamist rhetoric
adopted it against the solidarity manifested by the international
community. In these circumstances, far from renewing ties between
the two pillars of the West, September 11 and its aftermath have
continued to separate them. America and Europe have since then
been estranged as a result of a moral and psychological gulf in the
understanding of the event and its lessons, strategic differences as
to the evaluation of the threat and responses to be made to it, and
political divergences on the legitimacy of the extension of the war
against terrorism beyond the Islamist networks, particularly to

Iraq. Fukuyama himself now does not hesitate to speak of "fissures in the Western world."[3]

New Commandments for the Alliance

And yet, the shattering of the world evident in the ruins of the Twin Towers has made transatlantic solidarity and its restoration on new foundations more necessary than ever. This view is easier to defend from a European than from an American perspective because of Europe's obvious dependence on the United States. Now, as during the Cold War, Europe relies for its security primarily on NATO and the United States. It may be argued that the development of the European Community has established lasting peace on the continent, that the Soviet threat has disappeared, and that no other hegemonic power is likely to take its place. This fortunate development has, in fact, led to the massive withdrawal of American troops from European soil, reduced from 350,000 to 35,000 since 1991, and to the demotion of Europe from the category of strategic priority for the United States, which it had occupied for decades. As we have seen, the establishment of almost complete peace on its territory and its inability to participate in a significant way in the preservation of world security has led to the marginalization of Europe in the new American geopolitical perspective and its replacement by Russia, Israel, China, Turkey, India, and other strategic countries.

For all that, and contrary to the dominant feeling in Europe, the Old World is no less vulnerable and exposed than the New to terrorist threats, on its own territory and around the world. The wars in Bosnia and Kosovo showed that Europe was in no position to preserve peace on its frontiers without American intervention. If a European September 11 were to occur, it would no doubt cause the European members of NATO to invoke the military-assistance clause of the North Atlantic Treaty in order to call upon American aid. As the attacks in Bali and Yemen in the fall of 2002 confirmed, European security is also at stake in distant theaters—the Middle

East, Central and Southeast Asia, and Africa—where the EU has even less capacity for independent military intervention. And while it must in the future strive to reduce that dependence, Europe will be unable to do so unless it increases its contribution to collective security in partnership with the United States.

The situation is not fundamentally different in the economic realm, where, despite the single market and the success of the euro, Europe remains dependent on America with regard to its growth rate, the level of confidence of its economic actors, and the daily fluctuations of its stock markets. The decisions of the Federal Reserve's Open-Market Committee or even the statements of its chairman, economic statistics published in Washington, and the performances of Wall Street all condition the fluctuations in economic activity throughout Europe. Beyond economic interdependence and trade relations, this is due in part to the difficulty that the fifteen member states of the EU have had in pursuing European economic integration, particularly in the areas of banking and finance, in order to establish a vast domestic market comparable to that of the United States. In addition, the inability of prominent member states, particularly Germany and France, to initiate the structural reforms necessary to inject dynamism into the European economy, especially in fiscal and social matters, has resulted in an inadequate contribution by Europe to the stimulation of world growth. In the view of the G7 and the International Monetary Fund at the end of 2002, recovery can therefore come once again only from the United States because Japan has still not resolved the structural problems that its economy developed in the 1990s. Finally, like the rest of the world, Europe derives permanent benefit from the considerable contribution of the United States in scientific and cultural areas, such as art, education, and information. This contribution is ritually denounced as "American cultural imperialism," but it is nonetheless real and in fact much more accepted or even sought after than imposed.

While Europe thus has difficulty accepting its dependence on the United States, it is easy to see how the reverse holds even more strongly for the United States. The wars in Kosovo and Afghanistan showed that Europe had little to offer in the way of military contributions and especially that any joint intervention, through NATO or any other organization, was a source of political constraints and reduced effectiveness for America. Hence, in the aftermath of September 11 the United States stepped away from an alliance that historically had been dedicated to the defense of Europe and had been transformed by its enlargement to the east into an organization concerned more with political than with military cooperation. It nonetheless remains true that the United States has a strong need for Europe in other ways.

In the first place, the redeployment of American power on a global stage requires that Washington be able to rely increasingly on Europe for the latter's own security, which the United States now considers assured but in which it obviously must maintain a continuing interest. This concerns, of course, the Balkans and Eastern Europe, but not only those areas. America will thus have to support and foster the swift development of a European capacity for military intervention and its articulation with that of NATO. Second, politically even more than militarily, Europe is destined to make up the nucleus of shifting international coalitions, which the United States will need increasingly in order to legitimate its role as world policeman in the fight against new threats. The Iraqi crisis has shown that the political acceptability of American military intervention in the eyes of the world community was now critical for the United States, and France's successful strategy in the U.N. Security Council in the fall of 2002 confirmed the effectiveness of European-American understanding in bringing about a broader consensus, which was in turn a source of increased legitimacy, albeit temporarily. In the absence of constant support from the United Nations, which is difficult to guarantee, a closer partnership with the European Union would significantly attenuate the solitude of the single global power and the long-term political problem that that solitude poses for the United States.

Despite its sensitivities and its recurring denunciation of American oversimplifications and Manicheanism, Europe remains America's most solid ally. The entry of many nations into the post–September 11 antiterrorist coalition depended on opportunistic strategic considerations—dependence on Washington (Pakistan), threats to their own internal security (India, moderate Arab countries), legitimation of repression of domestic dissidents (Russia, China)—with little capacity to form the basis for deep and stable solidarity. The members of that coalition do not share the same fundamental interests, the same definition of terrorism, the same motivation, or, in any event, the same room for political maneuver to fight against it, not to mention their widely disparate records in respect of human rights. Fortunately, the community of values and of history that unites Europe with the United States is more than the mere convergence of immediate interests that America shares with many of its eastern allies. The European Union is therefore in a geopolitical environment that is, perhaps only temporarily, unipolar, the most reliable friendly restraint on the American superpower.

Finally, the United States has a great need of Europe in order to better understand the multipolar world of multiple civilizations outlined by Samuel Huntington and in order to find its way in the complicated East, which is more than ever the focus of the problems of world security. In the fight against terrorism the experience of European police, judicial, and intelligence organizations, as well as Europe's greater historical familiarity with Islam, have already been of great benefit to Washington. In the longer term, if openness and dialogue are to prevent the clash of civilizations, Europe, because of its history, its geographical location, its cultural diversity, its diplomatic positions, its sensitivity to the developing world, and the very experience of establishing European unity, is well po-

sitioned to show the way and to play a mediating role in the difficult dialogue between Washington and the "international community." Finally, the preservation of a strong link to old Europe
seems essential to preserve America's roots in Western civilization
and its Mediterranean cradle in the face of the geographical, economic, and cultural attraction, relayed by immigration and economic exchanges, of the Pacific and Latin American zones of influence and the spread of multiculturalism within American society
itself.

But the mutual dependence between Europe and the United
States is not the only reason for restoring transatlantic ties on a
lasting basis. Those ties are, in addition, a crucial factor for balance,
progress, and peace in the world. Beyond its economic and social
aspects, globalization means in effect that most of the great challenges facing the world—the protection of the environment and
sustainable development, public health, the fight against poverty
and malnutrition, education, economic and financial regulation,
the prevention of nuclear proliferation and terrorism—now have a
global character, in the twofold sense that they concern all humanity and can only be dealt with by broad international cooperation. This cooperation will have real chances for success only if
it is instituted under the shared sponsorship of the two most prosperous and influential democratic ensembles of the planet. Beyond
its strategic capacities, the United States must contribute its financial power, its educational, scientific, and technological resources, and its economic dynamism; and Europe must provide its
political vision, its public-service culture, its sensitivity to the problems of development, and its experience of multilateralism. Only
the combination of these attributes within a renewed alliance can
stimulate a new dynamic in postwar international organizations,
open up new roads to cooperation for the resolution of major world
problems, and take up the principal geopolitical challenges of the
next half-century, namely, a longstanding resolution of the Israeli-
Palestinian conflict, the integration of the Arab-Muslim world into

economic and democratic modernity, the rescue of the African continent, and the preservation of stability in a fast-changing Asia.

The Meaning of a Fight

In a broader historical perspective, the strengthening of transatlantic solidarity seems quite simply indispensable for the perpetuation of the Western legacy and its contribution to the recognition
of a set of universal values in a world that flouts them every day.
The discourse on the "defense of the West" certainly carries largely
negative political overtones in the history of international relations.
It evokes the Crusades, the arrogant domination of Christian Europe over Islam and the East, colonization and an ethnocentric pre-
sumption of superiority over devalued indigenous cultures, and finally the exploitation of the South by the North. Because of the
combined European and Asian character of the Soviet empire, for
several decades the Cold War replaced the historical burdens of the
Occidental-Oriental split with the simple geographical opposition
between East and West. But the fall of communism and the rise of
identity politics and fundamentalism have reestablished, for worse
rather than for better, cultural and religious issues at the heart of
international relations, at the very moment when the Western
frame of mind was becoming increasingly agnostic and permissive,
even setting up diversity and multiculturalism as supreme values,
particularly in America. The earthquake of September 11 and Islamist radicalism are part of that profound regression. While the
trap of a conflict of civilizations between Islam and the West must
be, and until now generally has been, avoided, there is no denying
that Islamist terrorism threatens the most fundamental values of
humanity and that those values have been articulated mainly by
Western civilization.

Excessively focused on creating false ethical and ideological divisions across the Atlantic, Europe's intelligentsia has rarely set itself on this universalist plane, probably because decades of Marx-
ist ascendancy had made the very concepts of "universality," "the

West," and "values" suspect and politically incorrect. In response to the worldwide accusations against their country, sixty American scholars of all political and ideological tendencies took the trouble to formulate, in a joint letter to the world, the philosophical and moral foundations for America's fight against terror.[4] Far from opposing one civilization to another, terrorism desecrates universal values defended by every civilization, including Islam: the sacredness of life and of human dignity; the prohibition of violence, even when religiously inspired; the existence of undeniable moral truths; the need for tolerance, pluralism, and neutrality in order to debate them; freedom of opinion, of religion, and of expression; and the legal equality of all mankind and between the sexes.

These values come of course from the Judeo-Christian tradition, and it is clear that the West has gone the farthest in developing them in political and legal terms, in a historical process rich in contradictions and regressions that nevertheless produced the Old and New Testaments, Greece and Rome, the Renaissance and the Reformation, skepticism and tolerance, capitalism and Marxism, democracy and human rights, Europe and America. The political progress of humanity since the seventeenth century has made possible the organization of international relations around legal principles derived from those same values, giving rise to a law of nations increasingly demanding of governments. Finally, in the course of the second half of the twentieth century this evolution was extended into the development of an international humanitarian law and the promotion of democracy and human rights against *raison d'état* around the world.

But this heritage should in no way confine the process and the values underlying it to the West alone, just as the rejection of a war between civilizations should not merely exonerate other cultures and religions from any responsibility for the proliferation of fundamentalism and terrorism. On the contrary, the call for dialogue must be tied to a stronger demand by the international community, led by Europe and the United States, for the implementation of

and respect for common values and the obligations that flow from
them by all the nations and civilizations on the planet, both in international relations and with respect to their own citizens. On this
depends the future of freedom and development in the world, perhaps the future of humanity itself. Huntington and Fukuyama con-
cur here with respect to the existence of values that are relevant to
all civilizations and are embodied today, philosophically, politically,
and legally, in human rights and liberal democracy, as evidenced in
the Universal Declaration of Human Rights. In this essentially normative sense Fukuyama can legitimately hold to his position;[5] his
thesis of the victory of liberal democracy seems, moreover, to have
been confirmed by some specialists on Islam in whose eyes, paradoxically, the fundamentalist revolution is behind us.[6]

    In the face of this demand for progress and universality, history
nevertheless constantly reminds us that what we now consider irreversible—freedom, democracy, the market economy, scientific
and technological progress—was the fruit of a long and tumultuous
struggle in the West. Every day the news demonstrates that what
we rightly consider to be universal values are of no benefit to the
majority of the world's population, that they constitute at best a set
of categories that have been more or less thoroughly assimilated in
Westernized civilizations, at worst the target of political and religious varieties of fundamentalism hostile to the West, and most
frequently a body of beliefs foreign to entire nations. An analysis
of the world's demographic, economic, and geopolitical prospects
points to the ineluctable rise of the economic, political, and military power of China, in Asia and beyond, the strengthening of various schools of Islam as a major political and religious force from
the Mediterranean to the Pacific, the proliferation of sources of
conflict between non-Western nuclear powers, the demographic
explosion of poor countries, and the preservation of a high con-
centration of the world's wealth within Western societies representing an ever decreasing fraction of the world's population.
These underlying tendencies foster the increasing vulnerability of

the West through waves of immigration encouraged by globalization and European integration, as well as through shifting economic and military hierarchies and now mass terrorism.

If the vision of a clash of civilizations should not serve to inflame tensions between East and West, North and South, the condemnation of this antagonism should not obscure the proliferation and intensification of attitudes hostile to Western philosophical and political values and the formidable regression that this development constitutes against the background of the harmony that was characteristic of the Mediterranean for centuries or, more recently, in comparison with the major internationalist advances of the twentieth century. The real challenge to the West, which is still in a position of strength, therefore consists in adopting a balanced attitude that is both open and firm toward the various forms of more or less violent attack to which the values it embodies are exposed around the world. The United States can rightly be criticized for responding to this complex challenge essentially in military and security terms, but Europe in turn must answer the charge of naïveté and irrelevance. Once again, the restoration of transatlantic relations on new foundations seems crucial for reaching a proper balance between these two attitudes and for providing answers to the planet's problems commensurate with the resources and the prosperity of the West. In this effort the West should receive increasing support from the developing world as terrorism intensifies its ravages on the economies of the South through the decline in investments and tourism and the increased difficulty in immigrating to Western countries.

This objective presupposes that Europe will add to its economic weight and its political good intentions a responsible diplomacy and a strategic capability commensurate with its responsibilities and ambitions and that the United States, beyond military force and in harmony with Europe, will fully assume its global leadership in every domain, economic, social, and ecological. A necessary step for calming tensions between civilizations and for the fight against new forms of totalitarianism, the establishment of more balanced transatlantic relations thus requires a new attitude on the part of both Europe and the United States toward the rest of the world.

The challenge appears to be a considerable one for both protagonists.

Chapter 4

EUROPE
IN SEARCH OF POLITICAL WILL
AND REPRESENTATION

Let us begin with old Europe and its position in the world. Since the failure of the premature plan for a European defense community in 1954, Europe's inability to play a significant diplomatic and strategic role on the world stage has been a fundamental weakness in the process of European unification. Years ago already, Henry Kissinger had a point when he inquired about the telephone number of his virtual counterpart in Europe. The accession of the EEC and then of the European Union to the status of a world political power has, however, always been considered a key goal of an enterprise established on the basis of economic integration that has enjoyed considerable success in its initial areas of competence—the single market, an international trade policy, and the recently established single currency. Reaching to the heart of national sovereignty and national sensitivities, foreign and security policies in fact represent the final frontier of the European project and the chief bone of contention in the traditional argument between defenders of Europe as an essentially economic organization, "Europe-space," and supporters of Europe as a political power, "Europe-power." The former, consistently led by Great Britain, would prefer to remain within a union with essentially economic aims

supplemented by intergovernmental political cooperation; the latter, under the ambiguous leadership of France, would like to make
Europe a political player on the world stage in keeping with its economic power. The opposition does not, however, completely co-
incide with the conflict between "federalists" and "sovereignists":
the supporters of Europe as a power are themselves divided between promoters of increased integration of European foreign and
security policies and defenders of an intergovernmental approach
to these questions for the foreseeable future. Attachment to national
sovereignty, as well as realism, places France in the second camp.

These different attitudes, however, share a linear vision of the
construction of Europe, designed to move gradually from economic matters to monetary ones, from the monetary to the political, and finally from the political to diplomacy and defense, these
last representing merely the most difficult stage to carry out. This
is indeed how the European project has progressed, from the initial Schuman Plan to the introduction of the euro fifty years later.
But the time has come to wonder whether this optimistic vision remains relevant and whether the persistent weakness of Europe in
diplomatic and military matters, far from representing the final
challenge to an ongoing process, is not rather a symptom of a larger
and deeper flaw. In the latter hypothesis—in support of which one
may mention the lack of political spillover effects so far following
the introduction of the euro—the aim of establishing Europe as a
power, even largely in an intergovernmental form, would be moving farther away rather than closer as the European Union changes
and expands, thus condemning the Old Continent to impotence
and irrelevance on the world diplomatic and strategic stage.

This fear is not new. For many years advocates of a Europe with
influence on the international stage have vainly called to the attention of heads of state and government the risk of dilution of this
objective posed by each succeeding enlargement. Many now de-
plore the victory of the British countermodel of a Europe reduced
to nothing more than a large economic and political organization

covering the entire continent, with no real external credibility. This reality has been obscured by the progress made since the Maastricht treaty in establishing a common foreign and security policy (CFSP) and, since December 1998, a European security and defense policy (ESDP). But these developments do not seem likely to change the underlying tendencies that, but for a qualitative shift that may eventually come out of the constitutional Convention on the Future of Europe, doom the European Union to marginality, particularly in its relations with the United States.

The Deconstruction of Europe

The development of European affairs in the last decade can be read in two diametrically opposed ways. The first emphasizes the advances made in the period: the single market and its external extensions in the areas of trade and competition policy, the successful introduction of the euro, a new major international currency competing with the dollar and the yen, progress in the areas of internal security and foreign and defense policy, the historic plan to reunify the continent by accepting ten new members from Central and Eastern Europe, and finally the prospect now coming to the fore of a real European constitution. This very positive view predominates outside the European Union, notably in the United States, where it inspires mixed feelings of admiration on the part of some and fear on the part of those who see the presumed rise in European power as antagonistic toward the United States, which is not illegitimate in the present context.[1]

That this optimistic analysis comes from distant observers in no way changes its relevance; on the contrary, like any view from outside, this one is correct on the essentials and is based on an appropriate time perspective, measured in decades. In this light, the construction of Europe constitutes an extraordinary political and geopolitical success that has insured peace, prosperity, and democracy in Western European nations and is preparing with the coming enlargement to take up a new, historic challenge. The

American salute is all the less surprising as the process has fulfilled
the expectations that motivated the support of successive postwar
administrations, from economic reconstruction, through Franco-
German reconciliation, to the containment of Soviet expansionism
and the permanent establishment of a market economy and the
rule of law from Brest to Warsaw (if not Vladivostok), culminating
in the reunification of the continent. The United States has real
grounds for complaint about Europe only in the realm of foreign
affairs, where it may legitimately criticize Europe's relative absence
and insignificance and denounce European ambivalence or even
hostility toward America.

The alternate reading of recent developments in European affairs, sharply more pessimistic, is concerned with the dynamics of
the political project itself and looks toward the future rather than
the past. This reading comes essentially from Europeans themselves, notably from those who have dedicated themselves to creating a political entity whose internal characteristics would be in-
separable from its existence on the international stage. In itself, this
pessimistic view does not contradict its counterpart, except that if
it were to be confirmed by the facts, it would not only limit the potential for European integration to its present stage of development
(which would satisfy the component of the American establishment
that is suspicious of it) but also likely undermine past accomplishments rightly acclaimed by international opinion.

Despite historical accomplishments and apparent good health,
the construction of Europe in fact dangerously regressed in the
1990s, at the very time when it was preparing to confront, with its
enlargement to twenty-five member states, an unprecedented
change in scale and in nature. This regression has two aspects: the
European Union accomplished nothing major after its creation in
the 1992 Maastricht treaty; even more seriously, it blindly forged
ahead at the risk of eventually compromising its effectiveness and
even its political relevance. The first assessment may seem surprising. However, economic and legal integration has marked time

since the inauguration of the single market on January 1, 1993. Economic and monetary union, the principal accomplishment of the period, was already conceived, programmed in detail, and approved in the Maastricht framework in 1992. As for political Europe, it has hardly fulfilled the promises that the sovereignists, fierce opponents of that treaty, presented as so many threats.

There are many reasons for this stagnation, but they have resulted in a slowing down of the engines that ensured the success of the European enterprise in the first four decades of its existence. The European Commission, guardian of the common interest and the only body with the power of initiative, never really recovered from the attacks to which it was subject during the campaigns for ratification of the Maastricht treaty, notably in France and Germany. Since then it has been internally weakened and strictly taken in hand by member states on the one hand and the European Parliament on the other, even in the economic realm, over which it has the broadest jurisdiction. The Court of Justice, the other historic engine for European integration, has gone through a comparable evolution for the same reasons.

But this takeover of the European process by member states has not given Europe an alternative dynamic. Quite the contrary, the French-German tandem, which from the beginning propelled the movement, has significantly loosened as a result of the German reunification, France's polite silence on several occasions in response to German proposals for a federalist evolution of Europe, and the new geopolitical context created by the end of the Cold War and economic globalization. These factors have been supplemented by the coming to power of new generations of national leaders who lack the European faith and sensitivities of their predecessors and for whom Europe is primarily a matter of necessity, pragmatism, and compromise among national interests. In this general context, reflecting a change in priorities for the larger countries, the addition of three new members in 1995 and the dilution of the original "Community method"[2] into a loosely defined union that is deprived of any legal personality and whose procedures are primarily intergovernmental fostered stagnation and regression.

In fact, the major act of the 1990s was the enlargement of the EU with the addition of Austria, Sweden, and Finland in 1995, to be followed by ten new members from Eastern and Central Europe in 2004.[3] Announced as early as the European Council in Lisbon in June 1992 to counterbalance the Danish rejection of the Maastricht treaty, the opening of membership to the East was responsive to a historical necessity and a moral debt toward the half of the continent abandoned to communism at the end of the war. The compatibility of this great project with the preservation of the no less important accomplishments of Europe over the course of the preceding forty years nevertheless required that the then twelve member states strengthen the institutions and decision-making procedures of the European Union before doubling its size. But nothing of the kind happened, and as various attempts at "deepening" the Union failed, enlargement began to look like a blind march forward, threatening to become a time bomb. From the preparation for the enlargement to fifteen, through the failure of the intergovernmental conference of 1996 and the inadequacy of the Amsterdam treaty, to the deplorable treaty of Nice, as labored as it is empty, the member states have shown themselves structurally unable to carry out the institutional reforms that would have enabled the European Union to take up the unprecedented challenge posed, because of their number, their heterogeneity, and their individual characteristics, by the integration of the nations of Central and Eastern Europe. Knowing that the European institutions are already no longer functioning with fifteen member states and that the adjustments made at Nice in view of the larger Europe are pointing in the wrong direction, one can only fear that a Union of twenty-five or thirty members will bear a strange resemblance to the defunct League of Nations.[4]

This failure is not fortuitous. Beyond a collective lack of vision on the part of heads of state and government, it reflects the disappearance of the "community spirit" that had enabled Europeans to overcome the wounds of history and divergent national interests for forty years. Beyond the consequences of an inadequately controlled enlargement, the deconstruction of Europe can be seen primarily in the return of national egoism and the absence of a common project for fifteen, much less twenty-five, nations. The observation that the emperor had no clothes became so obvious after the Nice debacle of December 2000 that the European leaders finally resigned themselves to entrusting the Continent's future to a prestigious political assembly—the Convention on the Future of Europe, presided over by former French president Valéry Giscard d'Estaing—whose mandate, in addition to writing a constitution, was nothing less than the rebuilding of the European project on realistic bases.

After fifty years of existence, and despite its formidable success in the realms of the economy, trade, and monetary unification, the European Union is thus having difficulty facing the challenge of its accession to the status of a strategic player on the world stage. It is against this background that the setbacks the Fifteen have so far experienced in their attempts to implement a common foreign and security policy can be properly understood.

Small-Steps Diplomacy

The development of a European diplomacy and defense policy has so far gone through three principal phases. Until the creation of the European Union by the Maastricht treaty, the incursions of the EEC into the diplomatic sphere were expressions of intergovernmental political cooperation lacking a specific institutional base. Diplomacy, therefore, remained national and was essentially the business of France and the United Kingdom, both nuclear powers and permanent members of the U.N. Security Council. In the military realm, American protection against the Soviet threat within the framework of NATO reduced the notion of unified European defense to a matter of mere debate, with London in firm and constant opposition to any formal link between European Community institutions and the security of the Continent.

The situation changed in 1993 with the treaty on the European Union, which added to the EEC two sovereign "pillars"—justice and internal affairs (JIA) and CFSP—intended to inaugurate Europe's entry into the political sphere. To be sure, the way in which these new powers were to be exercised remained intergovernmental, but at least they became subject to institutionalized policies of the European Union, capable eventually of evolving into a more integrated manner of operation along the lines of other European Community policies. Throughout the 1990s, marked by the dramatic conflicts in the former Yugoslavia, the concrete effects of the CFSP, as well as of police and criminal justice cooperation, were, however, rather slender, disappointing the expectations raised by the Maastricht treaty. Strategically, the end of the Cold War relaunched the old debate on the "European pillar" of a NATO in search of new purposes, but French and German attempts to establish this pillar on the basis of the venerable Western European Union once again came up against a British veto.

The third phase of European development in diplomacy and defense, initiated by the 1997 Amsterdam treaty, was on the contrary marked by a series of significant institutional and political advances. The new treaty created the post of high representative for CFSP, invented by France, intended finally to give a face to Europe in the international arena. It also institutionalized the mechanism of "enhanced cooperations," allowing a group of member states to move forward on integration in a specific area if they so wished without being blocked by recalcitrant member states. Saluted as a real turning point in European defense policy, the Franco-British summit at Saint-Malo (France) in December 1998 was notable chiefly for the end of Britain's persistent opposition to the establishment of a European defense independent from the United States. This change was no doubt facilitated by France's rapprochement with NATO, begun by Jacques Chirac in 1995. But it seems even more to have been the consequence of the gap in military capabilities on the two sides of the Atlantic, revealed by the Alliance's interventions in the Balkans, which called NATO's survival into question even in the eyes of the British. By advocating the implementation of an "autonomous" political and military capability by the European Union, the Franco-British declaration of Saint-Malo satisfied Washington's growing demands for "burden sharing" in European security and by the same token validated, thirty years later, the Gaullist argument that a strictly European defense would be a positive contribution to the solidity of the Atlantic Alliance. The "European Security and Defense Policy" (ESDP) was born.

At the European Council meeting in Cologne in June 1999 the European Union thus adopted the institutional framework necessary for political decision making on security and defense questions. Six months later in Helsinki the decision was made to create by 2003 a "rapid reaction force" of sixty thousand troops, able to intervene at short notice to carry out independently all the "Petersberg" missions (named after the German city where the European Council defining them had been held), that is, missions related to peacekeeping, crisis management, and humanitarian intervention. These developments and their implementation in the period 1999–2002 produced intense activity in foreign ministries, in European institutions, and among experts, creating the impression of significant progress in ESDP. This impression, however, has turned out to be generally illusory, particularly since September 11, 2001.

The continuing absence of Europe from a world diplomatic stage that has been rich in dramatic events in the last few years, notably in the Middle East, illustrates this illusoriness. Although it finances the Palestinian Authority to the tune of 250 million euros a year, the EU has no more influence over it than it does, more understandably, over the Israeli side. In the Iraqi crisis, it has stood out by virtue of its absence and then its bitter divisions. On the level of farce, when Morocco and Spain needed to settle their highly strategic quarrel over Parsley Island in the Strait of Gibral-

tar in July 2002, they called on Secretary of State Colin Powell
rather than on his closest European counterpart, Javier Solana.
The evidence is even more devastating in the military realm,
where, not even mentioning the Afghan campaign, the Bosnia and
Kosovo crises revealed Europe's inability to intervene effectively
without the assistance of the United States even in crisis management and peacekeeping operations on its immediate periphery. It
may be objected that the advances made since Saint-Malo,
Cologne, and Helsinki are the most significant that have been
made for European defense in the last fifty years, that they have not
yet been implemented, and that the past cannot therefore predict
the future, but the argument is not convincing.

With respect to foreign policy, the institutional shortcomings
that are generally blamed for European failings have not yet been
overcome. The CFSP remains intergovernmental, that is, governed by the rule of unanimity among the fifteen, soon to be
twenty-five, member states. Despite the personal qualities of its
high representative, Europe still has no credible face on the world
diplomatic stage. On the contrary, the scattering of European representation among this new figure (who is also the secretary general of the EU Council of Ministers), European Commissioner for
External Relations Christopher Patten, the rotating presidency of
the European Union, the president of the European Commission,
and above all the heads of state and government of the "larger"
member states confuses the picture and gives rise to frequent
parochial disputes without responding to Henry Kissinger's witti-
cism of more than twenty years ago. Presented as a panacea, the
"enhanced cooperation" mechanism was accompanied by so many
requirements and exceptions in the treaties of Amsterdam and Nice
(particularly with respect to CFSP) that it has never really func-
tioned. As for the plethora of intergovernmental committees set up
in the framework of the ESDP, they have managed to transform
European defense into an introverted bureaucratic labyrinth wor-

thy of the League of Nations brilliantly derided by the French novelist Albert Cohen.[5]

But these institutional aspects are themselves merely excuses, concealing less and less successfully the underlying difficulty of defining a common foreign policy for what will soon be twenty-five member states with traditions, interests, statures, and ambitions that are as heterogeneous as possible on the question. How is it possible to reconcile the principled defense of sovereignty of some with the soft Atlanticism of others and the de facto neutralism of most? How could Europe have a foreign policy without first defining its strategic interests and, in particular, resolving the obvious contradiction between its dependence on and solidarity with the United States and its efforts to establish an identity based on difference and opposition to that same United States? Other than the welcome intensification of cooperation in police and criminal-justice matters inside the EU, the geopolitical divide of September 11, 2001, in its multiple aspects, has given rise to no fundamental discussion among Europeans, much less between Europeans and Americans, about the adoption of a common strategy in the face of the terrorist threat, the political and economic problems of the Arab world, or any other subject. In the area of security and defense the Fifteen remain free from any commitment to solidarity like the one instituted between members of NATO by Article 5 of the North Atlantic Treaty. If Europe does not speak with a single voice, it is first and foremost because it lacks any strategic concept other than the wish to be friend to all, and notably the protector of widows and orphans.

The debate provoked in the international community and at the United Nations by the Bush administration's determination to disarm Iraq and in passing to end the regime of Saddam Hussein is a perfect illustration of the difficulty of a European foreign policy, the prospects for which on this occasion have clearly regressed. As we have noted, Europe distinguished itself in this crisis first by its absence, then by its deep divisions, even though this debate was essential for world stability. Initially, the three principal international powers of the EU displayed their differences publicly, without the slightest consultation and with the prudent silence of their twelve partners. Between the total solidarity of London with Washington and the no less radical and questionable opposition of Berlin to any military intervention in Iraq, French diplomacy initially succeeded in carving out a narrow path leading to a reasonable compromise with the Bush administration in the form of U.N. Resolution 1441. It would have been far preferable, and no doubt more effective, if this had been the result of a concerted European position rather than an initiative of France alone, partially contradicting the positions of its two principal partners. Subsequently, the bitter European divisions that followed France's and Germany's decisions to counter, along with Russia, the United States' efforts to obtain U.N. support for military action in Iraq did even greater harm to Europe than it did to transatlantic relations. After the intense diplomatic battle over Iraq, it is harder than ever to imagine France and Britain giving up their permanent seats on the Security Council in favor of some unidentified European voice.

This underlying problem is coupled with the inadequacy of the EU's military capabilities. If Europe has an economic diplomacy, it is because of its importance in world trade and the legal instruments that it has adopted in that domain. Similarly, it cannot have a foreign policy without having the means of applying and enforcing it. But the rapid-reaction force agreed upon at Helsinki for 2003 will not, according to most experts, be operational for several years, and then at a cost that the Fifteen do not seem eager to incur. Further, this force that has been so praised will enable Europe to perform only limited missions, thereby providing additional justification for many European nations, including the future Union members of Central and Eastern Europe, to rely on the United States and NATO to assure their security. As for the "spirit of Saint-Malo," hailed by French diplomacy, it seems to have vanished in the storms following September 11 and the Iraqi crisis, which put an end for the foreseeable future to any realistic prospect of a strategic readjustment between Europe and America within NATO, while at the same time bringing London and Washington much closer together, and Paris and London much farther apart.

Idyllic Europe

Beyond these numerous handicaps, the fundamental question that has now become unescapable is that of Europe's relationship to power. As long as European unification had merely an economic content the question remained hypothetical, the basis for a rhetorical opposition between supporters of Europe as a power—in trade and currency matters but also as a political, diplomatic, and military actor—and guardians of Europe as essentially an economic area, who rejected that ambition. Even so, the concept of Europe as a power was in part a fantasy because, as we have seen, its principal promoters, the French, conceived of European defense and diplomacy only within a strictly intergovernmental framework that preserved national sovereignty, which comes close to being a contradiction in terms.

The course of European developments in the 1990s, however, substantially changed the terms of the debate. On the one hand, the transformation of the EEC into a "union" with an expressly political character, with a single currency and a common foreign and security policy, gave substance to the concept of Europe as a power, or it at least made the question of power inescapable for Europeans. On the other hand, the rather virtual character of the political steps taken at Maastricht, and especially the continuing enlargement of the EU, strongly compromised Europe's ability to assert itself on the world diplomatic and strategic stage; in this respect the turning point of Maastricht can legitimately be seen as a Pyrrhic victory.

The simplistic opposition between the French view of Europe as a power and the British view of Europe as a "space" has now been replaced by the reality of a much more complex interplay among three categories of participants. The first includes nations with a universalist calling, possessing a diplomatic tradition and strategic capabilities and having no intention of abandoning those assets for the benefit of Europe. The description fits Great Britain, of course, but also France, the two coming together in a shared vision of intergovernmental and primarily national diplomacy and defense, while differing in the closeness of their ties to NATO and the United States. At the opposite pole are nations lacking in diplomatic traditions and ambitions, indeed reluctant to intervene in world affairs even through the European Union. This category may well become a majority with the approaching entry of "smaller" Eastern European countries who will follow the 1995 admission of the traditionally neutral Austria, Sweden, and Finland. In between, some significant and not so significant nations—Germany, Italy, Spain, the Benelux states, and some of the Eastern newcomers—are inclined, to various degrees, to favor Europe's taking a more active role in world affairs but are not, for varying historical and political reasons, notably their relationship to the United States, able or willing to play a leading role in this area. The aversion of German public opinion to any use of force, for example, constitutes a substantial obstacle to any advance in establishing a common European defense based on a Franco-German partnership excluding Britain.

The consequence of this heterogeneity has not been, as is often thought, the establishment of the kind of free-trade area traditionally favored by the British—a concept that has been obsolete since Maastricht and the success of the euro—but, more perniciously, the institution of a very peculiar European attitude toward power and international relations. A kind of compromise has in fact been established between the declared ambitions of the treaty and the lack of will and ability on the part of most of the member states to turn the European Union into an actor on the world political stage. This compromise in the form of the lowest common denominator meant conferring on the EU the traits of a "civil power," with no calling to make war, only to work for conflict resolution and to keep the peace; with no expansionist aims or particular interests to defend outside its borders, only virtuous principles and practices to export onto the international stage. This philosophy has been formulated in many political declarations over the last few years and was reflected operationally in the articulation of the Petersberg missions—crisis-management and peacekeeping operations—serving as a guide for a (future) ESDP.

Very significantly, the French themselves, traditional promoters of Europe as a power, even with the ambiguities noted above, have changed their discourse.[6] Power has ceased to be a "politically correct" ambition for Europe since the term, with its Napoleonic overtones, frightens France's Irish and Scandinavian partners. In contrast to the "imperialism" attributed to American power, the international ambition of Europe is supposed to consist merely in "humanizing globalization," organizing the "governance" of the planet, helping to resolve crises on the EU's periphery, ensuring the preservation of peace, and attempting to export around the world its model of cooperation and legal and diplomatic resolution of disputes.

We should acknowledge from the outset that this "strategic doctrine" makes a good deal of sense for Europe. First of all, it has the advantage of being realistic: given their present political will and strategic capabilities, it is hard to see how the Europeans could credibly harbor a larger ambition. From the point of view of the larger countries, the concept of a "civil power" also makes it possible to justify the continuation of national foreign and defense policies, as well as ad hoc intergovernmental cooperation in military matters, because the EU has in a sense declared itself without jurisdiction in this area. More profoundly, the concept of a civil power stems directly from the historical experience and uniqueness of European unification, as well as from its diplomatic stance. This truly exceptional experiment consisted in establishing lasting and ever more widespread peace and prosperity on a continent that had been riven by war and had been the source of most regional and world conflicts for centuries. Its uniqueness is to have achieved this result, at least in part, by means of a novel and peaceful form of international relations, based on multilateral dialogue, institutions, law, and solidarity. This twofold miracle constitutes the singular and exemplary character of the construction of Europe within universal political history and the contemporary world order. It is thus altogether natural that Europeans should strive to project onto the world stage the virtues that have proved so successful for them.

This stance seems all the more appropriate in a world that is dominated by an increasingly inaccessible American power that is focused on the military and security dimensions of diplomacy and is autonomous in the conduct of its foreign policy. In the confrontation between the United States and the international community Europe has thus rediscovered the distanced attitude that it adopted between the two superpowers during the Cold War. Of course, it remains an ally of the United States, but an ally that is always inclined to emphasize its difference and to assume the position of a mediator for the benefit of the rest of the world—the nonaligned countries in the recent past, the "moderate" countries of the developing world today. This attitude has become even more advantageous since the end of the Cold War because it has enabled a Europe freed from the Soviet threat to oppose American power in terms almost as Manichean as those attributed to George W. Bush's America: multilateralism versus unilateralism, negotiation versus military intervention, law versus force, peace versus war . . .

The problem is that this vision of the world suffers from two major errors in perspective that no European leader can ignore. The first has to do with the historical conditions that have permitted the existence, and especially the success, of Europe unification itself. That success owes a good deal, notwithstanding the undeniable virtues of the elites and the populations involved in bringing it about, to the United States' initial encouragement and continuing goodwill at the political level, to the aid it provided for Europe's economic reconstruction, and to the military protection given through NATO. There can be little doubt that in the face of Soviet pressure, the absence of any of these conditions would have compromised any attempt at European unification.

This reminder is intended not so much to point to a debt owed to the United States as to shed light on the second error in perspective characteristic of current European idealism. Minimizing the substantial external contribution to their own accomplishments, Europeans take a further step into an illusory world by imagining that they can reproduce their own regional success outside the West and that they can do this without, or even in opposition to, the United States. This thinking simply disregards the exceptionally favorable circumstances that fostered European unification, resulting as much from the American contribution as from the shared culture and historical experience of the nations of the Continent. Devastated and marginalized by the two world wars of the twentieth century, united by a common heritage, and protected by the American nuclear umbrella, Europe brought together the indispensable conditions for constructing a model of internal organization based on peace, law, solidarity, and compromise, in the philosophical tradition of Locke and Kant. Credit for this success belongs, of course, primarily to the Europeans themselves, but this does not mean that the experience can be extended to the international system as a whole or even that the virtuous practices involved in building Europe can be transposed to the chaotic world of the twenty-first century. This world is the opposite in every respect of the European paradise: It has no cultural cohesion, no shared desire to exorcise a bloody past, no tradition of the rule of law, and no universal military guarantee. On the contrary, it is characterized by a discontinuity of cultures, if not a clash of civilizations, a proliferation of threats, notably "asymmetrical" ones, virulent varieties of nationalism, a lack of democratic traditions, and the worst violations of human rights.

In a brilliant and stimulating article that set many teeth on edge in Europe the neoconservative political scientist Robert Kagan attributes the current strategic divorce between Europe and the United States to two factors.[7] First, the growing disparity in military capabilities on the two sides of the Atlantic, obscured by the centrality of Europe to the stakes of the Cold War, has produced a corresponding divergence between the strategic views and attitudes of the two protagonists toward power. Whereas the Americans, in a dominant position in an ever more turbulent and hostile world, seek to maintain order, by force if necessary, the Europeans, in a position of weakness, wish to build a world from which force would be banished and would thereby become useless. From this point of view, the Bush administration's unilateralism and militarism constitute factors upsetting to the world order advocated by Europeans.

But Kagan refines the analysis further by observing a kind of reversal of roles in the development of different strategic cultures on the two sides of the Atlantic. While the United States has moved from the Wilsonian idealism and internationalist legalism that it embodied for most of the twentieth century to the unilateralist realpolitik of the last decade, the Europeans have traveled the opposite path. With the construction of the European Community and the resolution of the "German question," they have turned their backs on centuries of power politics and traded Machiavelli and Hobbes, Napoleon and Bismarck, for Locke's faith in the peacemaking virtues of trade and the Kantian ideal of perpetual peace. While the American Leviathan, because of its very power and the hatred that it provokes, has seen itself increasingly forced to live in the real world of the "clash of civilizations" and has adapted its strategic culture as a result, Europe has been living for the past fifty years in the postmodern utopia of its own unification and is dreaming, without fully admitting it, of the end of history for all. Having abandoned force and power as guiding principles in international relations internally, Europe could not possibly adopt them in its relations with the rest of the world, America included, which it is attempting to convert to its new catechism. Of course, the military gap and the ideological divide are mutually reinforcing, with the ideological dismissal of power justifying the lack of any serious defense effort and the resulting vulnerability in return underlining the necessity for a pacifist stance on the part of Europe and an increasingly firm denunciation of the martial unilateralism of the United States.

Kagan's analysis may be considered provocative and reductive, but it came as a salutary wake-up call for the Europeans. The Old Continent still runs the risk of waking up one morning to the recognition that the world is not the way it would like it to be, that this is not entirely the fault of American "imperialism," that the principles and ideals that have governed the construction of Europe have not immunized it against the hatred that the West inspires, and that America will not necessarily always be there to protect it. It is already clear in the Middle East and elsewhere that Europe's strategic weakness denies it any serious influence in world affairs, even on the rare occasions when it has a specific message to deliver. In its chosen areas of "global governance" and development aid, its generosity toward the developing world in international trade negotiations remains relative, and it has yet to establish an independent capability to intervene in peacekeeping operations. Much more seriously, its irrelevance in world geopolitics is in the process of compromising, even for public opinion and for its most fervent supporters, the credibility of a political project that remains one of the most impressive successes in the history of civilization. Indeed, how is it possible to continue to defend and promote the construction of Europe in the face of the growing disappointment that its role in, and stance toward, the world have provoked? In its own interests, even more than in the interests of its relationship with the United States, the European Union must therefore add to its multilateralist culture, which is now its distinctive contribution on the world stage, a genuine strategic dimension, which alone can strengthen its credibility.

The Great Leap Forward

In the world after September 11, Europe finds itself more than ever
before at a crossroads.[8] It can continue on its current course, by
striving to set up the rapid-reaction force decided on in Helsinki
in 1999, to complete its extension to the East and to make marginal
improvements, through a constitution, in the effectiveness, trans-
parency, and democratic legitimacy of its mode of operation. In this
scenario, which is the most likely one, its contribution to world stability will be far from negligible. It will consist first of all in having established lasting peace and prosperity on a continent that was
historically the principal source of international conflict. If we re-
call that the neutralization of Europe as a factor of worldwide in-
stability, even if that meant its marginalization, was among the
strategic objectives of the United States in the interwar period, the
European Union represents a dignified version of that rather emas-
culating project.[9] By gradually extending its benefits to the south
and then to the east of the continent the EU has in addition made
a substantial contribution to the extension of democracy and the
market economy, as well as to the international order of the
post–Cold War world. In this sense the process of enlargement can
be considered the keystone of Europe's foreign policy so far. Finally, if the EU gives itself the military means to resolve independently the political crises that may arise on its territory or on
its immediate periphery—which one hopes will be increasingly
residual—it will thereby have taken full responsibility for the security of the second most important political community on the
planet and to that extent relieved the United States. Such an
achievement would be considerable, even though the continent is
largely pacified by now.

This scenario means, however, that Europe would continue to
depend essentially on American military protection in case of a serious external challenge to its own security and that it would be
barred from playing a significant role in world affairs, both for want

of strategic capability and because its vulnerability would prohibit it from adopting too militant a stance in the face of new threats. The United States would thus continue to assume alone the thankless and dangerous role of world policeman, with European assistance in peacekeeping operations. This choice requires at the very least a clarification for public opinion of the strategic ambitions of the EU and more importantly a significant tightening of the relationship with the American ally. Nothing could in fact be more damaging to transatlantic relations and for the future security of the continent than a Europe that was seen by the United States as simultaneously irrelevant, irresponsible, and ungrateful.

But this is precisely the crux of the matter. How is it possible to establish lasting harmony, in the context of a serious international crisis (Iraq being a case in point), between solidarity with Washington and "neutralization" of the EU's foreign policy? Does that stance not presuppose at least a certain distancing from an often bluntly conducted American foreign policy? If Europe favors the latter attitude and continues its balancing act, its relationship with Washington will further deteriorate. If, on the contrary, it gives priority to transatlantic solidarity, its neutralist posture will suffer and the United States will in addition and rightly ask it to take on a more significant portion of the financial and military burdens of international security. It is clear, however, that this latter path is the only one consistent with the fundamental interests of the West as a whole, and the only one worthy of, and consistent with, the frequently asserted ambition of seeing the EU play its role in world affairs and making its difference from the United States heard. This is only an apparent paradox: only by ending its status as a free rider on American power can Europe simultaneously remove one of the underlying obstacles to an intra-European agreement on a common foreign and security policy, strengthen its credibility in the eyes of the international community, win acceptance for its diplomatic vision, and thereby influence the foreign policy of its powerful ally.

The damage caused to European unity by the Iraqi crisis of early 2003 could provide a fresh opportunity to carry out the historic shift that Europe's rediscovery of power would represent. The word *power* should not cause fear: between the "superpower" of America that Europe does not want, even if it could have it, and its current weakness, there is a middle ground that should make it possible for Europeans to take care of their own security, protect their interests and win acceptance for their views in the world, and contribute more to the preservation of collective security alongside the United States. After the shock of September 11, 2001, this was one of the principal challenges facing the unprecedented political experiment of the Convention for the Future of Europe, conceived of as a means for giving new impetus to the European project. Since Islamist hyperterrorism has made its appearance, matters of domestic and external security and foreign and defense policy have rightly become dominant concerns for the population of Europe. This decisive development has, however, found no adequate response among the heads of state and government of the fifteen member states. The French presidential and legislative elections in the spring of 2002 took place without the slightest debate on the future of Europe, the international situation, or even national security in the context of September 11, 2001. Germany did slightly better with the sudden emergence of the Iraqi question in the campaign, but the electoralist opportunism and the verbal excesses of Gerhard Schröder's team took the country in the wrong direction.

In the convention presided over by Valéry Giscard d'Estaing, debates on these subjects have been too restricted to institutional matters, and debates on such issues have never contributed much to progress in this area: Can foreign and security policy be governed under European Community rules, or must they remain intergovernmental? Are they destined to be a matter of "enhanced cooperation" or of a "core" grouping together countries interested in them? If so, with which participants, and according to which rules? The reason for this marching in place, eerily disconnected

from international reality, is, as always, the inability of the Fifteen
to deal with the underlying lack of a common project and of comparable ambitions and capabilities among the various member
states, particularly in these areas. As though this were not sufficiently immobilizing, this heterogeneity is coupled, as we have
seen, with ambivalence on the part of the countries principally concerned with foreign and security policy (the United Kingdom,
France, Germany, and a few others) toward their own level of ambition for Europe and the articulation of a possible European
strategic capability with national sovereignty and with transatlantic
relations. The end of this ambivalence by means of a significant political and budgetary commitment, at least on the part of those
countries, is unquestionably a prerequisite for any progress toward
a unified European diplomacy and defense policy.

However important they may be, institutional solutions cannot
in fact replace a basic agreement on the purposes, ambitions, and
broad outlines of a foreign policy for Europe, nor can they even pre-
cede such an agreement. On the contrary, after years of immobility,
it is now legitimate to believe that only such an agreement could
open the way to an institutional compromise on decision-making
procedures in this area. When two corporations decide to create a
joint subsidiary for which each will surrender independent decision-
making capacity, it is customary for them to define contractually in
advance the outlines of the subsidiary's policies. If they are unable
to do so, they generally give up their plans. What is valid in the
world of business is also valid, *mutatis mutandis*, in European affairs.

From this perspective one might imagine, long after the Iraqi
dust has settled, a "critical mass" of member states, assembled
around the Paris-London-Berlin triangle, solemnly declaring that
an economic and political entity as important as the European
Union cannot dispense with an autonomous strategic and defense
capability sufficient to stand behind an external policy whose major
axes have not been fully defined by the fine words of the past ten
years. Such a policy should be based on the identification of a few

major strategic interests specific to Europe, beyond simple principles and ideals of supposedly universal application. Formulating
such a definition, outside the sphere of the economy and trade, is
certainly a difficult exercise for several reasons. First of all, after a
half-century of American military protection followed immediately
by the illusions of the post–Cold War period, the governments and
peoples of Europe are not prepared for it. For the purposes of this
exercise, the nations of Europe should think of themselves as lacking NATO's permanent military guarantee but nevertheless as
strong enough to defend their interests appropriately and to take
care of their own security. In addition, the consciousness of external European political interests presupposes a clear distinction between "internal" and "external," which leads us back to the current
uncertainty about the geographical and cultural borders of the EU,
with Turkey as a test case, and even more fundamentally to the difficult gestation of a European political and strategic identity.

Despite this twofold difficulty, it should be possible to articulate
Europe's strategic interests around a few major axes, consisting of
the internal and external security of the Union, its member states,
and its allies; the stability of its eastern and southern borders; the
protection of its economic and commercial interests, as well as of
its cultural identity; and, more traditionally, the promotion of its
values and of the multilateral system in the service of peace, development, and democracy in the world. On the basis of this essential platform, the determination of European interests would
develop pragmatically, along the lines of the famous definition of
pornography given by U.S. Supreme Court Justice Potter Stewart:
"I know it when I see it."[10] Transposed to the more austere domain
of international relations, this means that the external affairs that
will be of interest to Europe as such will stand out as those about
which Europe's absence or silence is now generally deplored either
because its strategic, political, or economic interests are at stake
or—and the two are not incompatible—because it has a specific
contribution to make to a crisis situation in which it is not directly

involved. On such questions, and in spite of Iraq, it is reasonable to believe that a genuine political will, taking into account the diversity of national sensitivities, would be capable of bringing forth a common strategic vision.

On all international questions thus considered to be of European interest, and thereby coming principally under EU jurisdiction, the member states at the origin of this initiative would do their best to reach within a limited time a common position potentially leading to a military engagement. Only following, and in case of the failure of, such a process of consultation could member states that wished to do so resume their diplomatic and strategic freedom. On questions not of general European interest, on the other hand, member states specifically concerned would be free to intervene as they wished, provided they acted in overall accordance with the Union's external policy.

Once these rules of operation were established, the group of member states responsible for such an initiative would propose to their partners that the external policy and the strategic capacity so defined be assumed by the EU itself, under institutional, operational, and financial procedures to be specified, but of a kind that would enable Europe to swiftly attain credibility in this area. If this proposal were to meet rejection, with regard to the conditions for its implementation, by a critical mass of member states, then this European diplomatic and strategic capability would have to be established outside the EU, with the necessary corollary that the Union would give up its ambitions and its jurisdiction in these matters. This is not a desirable solution, because it presents the twofold disadvantage of dissociating economic and monetary power from military capacity and thereby requiring complex mechanisms to coordinate the two. If, conversely, the proposition of having Europe accomplish a qualitative leap in matters of foreign and security policy were to provoke the opposition of only a minority hardly likely to compromise its realization, recalcitrant member states should be invited to choose, in the higher interests of the Union, between abandonment of their opposition and relegation to the status of participants in the existing European Economic Area.

The approach just outlined is obviously "politically incorrect," schematic, and open to differing formulations and variations, but it is the only one that offers the possibility of escaping from the impasse in which European diplomacy and defense have languished since Maastricht, and it can therefore not be criticized as unrealistic. On the contrary, what appears unrealistic is the idea that in the geopolitical situation of the emerging twenty-first century a political and economic entity as important and prosperous as the European Union could live for long without a defense force or as a parasite of the United States, as well as the hope of building common foreign and defense policies among a majority of member states that want neither one. In the countries likely to spur this kind of clarifying process—principally France and the United Kingdom—the major obstacle, along with the Atlantic question, discussed in the final chapter, remains the sovereignist instinct, the desire to preserve national autonomy in diplomatic and strategic matters, a longstanding attitude now rightly reinforced, in light of the divisions over Iraq and the coming enlargement, by the fear of giving up real power for the illusion of an unlikely common policy.[11]

In response to this legitimate concern, one may argue that in diplomatic and strategic matters the European nation-states are now in a situation comparable to the one they were in with respect to monetary affairs ten years ago. No doubt the illusion of national sovereignty is easier to maintain in the symbolic order of foreign policy than in the reality of the markets, but this is less true in the area of defense, where it is clear to everyone that no European country, with the partial exception of the United Kingdom, can participate on its own in a military operation of significant size. The argument that supported the advent of the euro is thus now valid for defense and indirectly for foreign policy, given the developments in American doctrine and strategic capabilities. As for the danger of giving up the reality of national independence, however symbolic, for the shadow of a common European policy, it confirms once more the necessity for the broadest possible federalization of any responsibility taken on by Europe as a whole, with individual member states maintaining, in a subsidiary capacity, their national prerogatives in areas of external relations specific to them.

Only after these fundamental choices have been implemented can there be a fruitful discussion of the institutional arrangements, the military and industrial options, and especially the budgetary commitments needed to make European diplomacy and defense and transatlantic cooperation truly effective. Institutionally, Europe requires unity in its international representation and a decision-making capacity in external relations. This in turn requires a rationalization of the plethora of more or less rivalrous institutions, mostly intergovernmental, that now serve as a screen for European impotence. Measures on the agenda include the abolition of the rotating presidency of the Union in favor of a more permanent leadership and external representation; the combination in a single political post of international stature of the functions of high representative for CFSP and commissioner for external relations; and the coordination of actions undertaken for internal and external security. The CFSP and the ESDP are thus bound to open the way to a genuine European executive branch, which is now lacking in those areas, as in many others. The effectiveness of European trade and competition policies points to the ingredients needed for that purpose: exclusive community jurisdiction, integrated legal mechanisms, recognized and responsible authority.

Militarily, developments since September 11, 2001—the shift of American priorities away from Europe, the rapprochement between Washington and Moscow, the marginalization of NATO, and the disjunction between military capabilities on the two sides of the Atlantic—call for a reexamination of the objectives set out at Helsinki in December 1999 in light of the new division of responsibilities for collective security between the United States and Europe. In order to ensure the security of its own territory and that of its immediate periphery, the EU has to be in a position to carry out missions like the one in Kosovo without Washington's help, which presupposes that it will develop in the medium term independent military capabilities and autonomous planning. The creation of a European armed force, which is what is at stake, requires in turn a strong political impetus and continuing direction by heads of state and government, a budgetary commitment generally estimated at 2 percent of GDP, and coordination with NATO in order to ensure compatibility and "constructive duplication" between weapons systems.[12] This effort would require the consolidation of European defense industries in the framework of an armament policy, with a view toward counterbalancing the revival of the American military-industrial complex and facilitating the opening of defense markets on both sides of the Atlantic.

Finally, and above all, in the global struggle against new threats the European strategic effort must be thought of in terms of specialization and of complementing American and NATO capabilities. Considering its particular assets, its budgetary constraints, the nature of the threats, and Washington's emphasis on heavy equipment and technology, European defense policy would have every interest in specializing in "softer" areas, such as civil defense, intelligence, particularly human intelligence, special forces, and special operations relying on expertise, cultural permeability, and operational excellence, with all of which Europe may be better provided than the United States. Relatively inexpensive, this European specialization would nevertheless be of great usefulness alongside American hard and technological power in the fight against international terrorism in all its forms. Institutionally this orientation would be accompanied by the extension of the Petersberg missions to the fight against terrorism around the world and by a commitment to mutual help and solidarity inside the EU on matters of civil defense and internal security, as France and Germany jointly proposed at the close of 2002.

Only through efforts of this kind, and in the framework of fundamental solidarity with the United States, can Europe contribute usefully to the balancing of American power that it legitimately desires.

Chapter 5

AMERICA AND THE CHALLENGE
OF A NEW INTERNATIONALISM

Does America need a foreign policy? This provocative question serves as the title of Henry Kissinger's latest book, published in early 2001.[1] Contrary to what detractors of American "unilateralism" might imagine, Richard Nixon's former secretary of state did not intend to suggest that the United States could do without any kind of diplomacy but rather to denounce the lack of direction that has characterized Washington's foreign policy since the end of the Cold War. What was true before September 11, 2001, is a little less so today because America has found an alternative enemy, which has redefined its foreign policy. Nonetheless, engaged in a war against terrorism, the United States is still in search of a diplomacy capable of improving its relations with an international community that it can no longer do without.

The source of the paradoxes, contradictions, and structural dilemmas of American foreign policy, now at the center of its confrontation with the rest of the planet, lies in the Janus face of the United States, a democracy of near continental size, a peaceful trading nation, self-sufficient and introverted, but also first and now sole global power, engaged economically, diplomatically, and militarily in the four corners of the world. From this schizophrenic nature, which the French philosopher Raymond Aron summed up under the label "imperial republic," there follow a series of more or less problematic consequences.[2] On one side, foreign policy is of only minor interest to a public that is already relatively indifferent to federal concerns and principally focused on its immediate environment. Along with defense, foreign policy is thus the concern of a small circle of diplomats, military officials, and experts concentrated in Washington, whereas political figures in general are principally concerned with the local interests they represent at the federal level. Hence, foreign policy is often merely the international extension of domestic political concerns, particularly in matters of trade and the economy. Thus the protectionist measures adopted at various times by Washington, such as steel tariffs and farm subsidies, are the result of pressure from lobbies and the nearly permanent electoral concerns of the administration and Congress. The same holds true for America's rejection of certain international treaties, such as the Small Arms Treaty, held hostage by the National Rifle Association. Institutionally, the separation of powers between the executive and the legislature and the role of the Senate in the ratification of treaties, and of Congress as a whole in trade negotiations and the approval of military interventions, intensifies the dominance of domestic politics over foreign policy.

But on the other side, in the face of these hardly avoidable democratic exigencies, stand the realities of American power and influence in the world, which confer on many diplomatic decisions, and even some purely domestic ones, major international consequences. This is, of course, the case for Washington's positions in diverse multilateral contexts, and even more so in local and regional conflicts. In the economic realm, globalization has given American domestic decisions a de facto extraterritorial impact. A recent example is the applicability to foreign companies raising capital in the United States of the Sarbanes-Oxley legislation, adopted in the summer of 2002 in response to the financial and accounting scandals of the late 1990s.

The Sources of Unilateralism

The paradox of a giant turned in on itself whose slightest movements provoke worldwide aftershocks is at the heart of American diplomacy's historical dilemma, and its pendulum swings between isolationism and interventionism. For Hamilton, Jefferson, and Madison, American democracy was founded on principles and moral values far superior to those of the European monarchies in perpetual conflict. Its universal mission was to enlighten the world by its example and the perfection of its exceptionalism, while taking care to keep itself removed from the power struggles endemic to Europe and hoping that the powers of the Westphalian order would neutralize one another. Isolationism was thus coupled at first with the Messianism inherent in the American political tradition. In 1823 the formulation of the Monroe Doctrine, which strongly urged European nations, notably England and Spain, to keep out of the Americas, thenceforth the preserve of the United States, by the same token enabled the nation to take even less interest in the rest of the world. The nineteenth century was thus a century of American isolationism, of a near absence of foreign policy.

Theodore Roosevelt's assumption of office at the end of the Spanish-American War opened the twentieth century under the sign of a more classic conception of international relations, understood as the science of the balance of powers, but also under the sign of an interventionism unprecedented in the national tradition in order to preserve that balance. Initially defensive toward the European powers, the Monroe Doctrine was thus complemented by the assertion of the United States' right to intervene in the Western Hemisphere in order to protect its interests, a right that would be exercised on several occasions in the Caribbean and Central America. Above all, the United States thereafter took positions in conflicts between foreign powers, in Europe but also in Asia, as in the 1904 Russo-Japanese War and the 1908 Japanese invasion of Korea.

But Roosevelt's realpolitik motives soon gave way to Wilsonian idealism as a justification for the salutary intervention of the United States in the First World War and most subsequent conflicts. In fact, the United States' entry into the war in 1917 could hardly be legitimated by any threat to its national security, nor was it directed toward preserving European balance. On the contrary, it was in order to have done with the deadly games of the powers of the Old World and to impose a general peace that Woodrow Wilson committed America to war. This moral justification for interventionism was in fact more in keeping with the American political tradition than was Roosevelt's adoption of the European-style balance of power. Thus, American interventionism in the twentieth century derived from the same source as the isolationism of the preceding century, with the difference that America now intended to contribute positively to reshaping the world in its own image rather than merely preaching in the desert by example.

After the isolationist reaction of the 1920s, which had disastrous consequences for Europe, the universalist internationalism invented by Wilson was swiftly restored and shaped the foreign policy of the United States until the end of the Cold War. From Franklin Roosevelt through Truman, Eisenhower, and Kennedy to Ronald Reagan, the founding episodes of international relations in the twentieth century—the rise of totalitarianism and the Second World War, the construction of a new Western European, Atlantic, and international order after 1945, the East-West conflict—in fact fostered the alliance of idealism and realism, the synthesis of universalism and national interest, in the service of an active and internationalist diplomacy. Nazi Germany's domination of Europe, the Japanese attack on Pearl Harbor, the worldwide chaos resulting from the war, and especially Soviet expansionism sufficiently engaged U.S. interests to ensure the rallying of the isolationist camp to Rooseveltian interventionism, broadly appealing on the grounds of democratic values, collective security, and human rights. Finally, America came out of the war with enough power to reconstruct an international order according to its wishes and thus to reconcile universal values and national interests.

The bipartisan consensus that gave coherence to American foreign policy throughout most of the twentieth century by glossing over its internal tensions began to erode in the jungles of Vietnam before disappearing with the fall of the Berlin Wall. The collapse of the Soviet Union, consecrating the pacification and the reunification of Europe, also meant the disappearance of all threats to the security of the United States, a prerequisite to interventionism in the eyes of conservative Republicans. Despite the success of the Gulf War, George Bush lost the 1992 election on the basis of the economy. Throughout the 1990s the interventionism of the Clinton administration in Somalia, Haiti, Bosnia, and Kosovo was justified principally on humanitarian grounds, without the support of the Republican camp, which questioned its conformity with the national interest, with the notable exception of support for the Israeli-Palestinian peace process. Entirely taken up with celebrating the end of history and the new economy, America seemed less concerned than ever with foreign policy, to the great chagrin of figures like Henry Kissinger.

This is the general context in which we must analyze the diplomatic shift carried out well before September 11, 2001, by the new Republican administration, through denunciation of the muddled humanitarianism of the Clinton years, the announcement of American withdrawal from the Balkans, and a refocus on a more rigorous vision of the national interest. But times have changed, and in an era of globalization the isolationism of the nineteenth century is no longer appropriate for the only superpower on the planet. In these circumstances, the "unilateralism" so disparaged by the Europeans represents nothing but a natural synthesis, long latent but never expressed in the American diplomatic tradition, between the two historical poles of isolationism and interventionism, under the impact of a threefold change in the international system at work since the end of the Cold War.

The first component of this change is the globalization that has glibly been called "American," although the United States has not yet taken its full measure. This globalization has made it impossible for the United States to abstain from any aspect of world affairs, from events in the former Yugoslavia and the Horn of Africa to issues such as sustainable development and the terrorist threat, the "global" character of which has only reinforced Washington's necessarily worldwide involvement. On top of this first aspect of the new international system comes the strategic supremacy that America now holds on the world stage, which endows it with almost totally autonomous decision-making power. Finally and most important, the almost universal rise of anti-Americanism, embodied in extreme form by the September 11 attacks, constitutes a third powerful engine driving unilateralism. How can the United States resist the temptation to act according to its self-interest alone and in conformance with its own convictions when it has the means to do so, the certitude that it is defending a just cause and universal values, when it is the principal target of international terrorism and the object of worldwide hostility, and when, finally, it has no totally reliable and credible partner at its side?

A natural component of any foreign policy, unilateralism thus appears to be a fundamental aspect of the foreign policy of the principal world power in an era of globalization, unipolarity, and widespread anti-Americanism. While the diplomacy of George W. Bush represents the fullest expression so far of this unilateralism, the tendency also marked the positions of the Clinton administration—backed, it is true, by a Republican majority in Congress—toward several international treaties, including the treaty on antipersonnel mines, the Kyoto agreement on climate change, and the treaty establishing the International Criminal Court. The intensification of unilateralism carried out by the new administration is no doubt less the result of a traditional Republican attitude than of the impact and the consequences of September 11, which exacerbated the underlying reasons for that attitude.

The attacks against the World Trade Center and the Pentagon first of all tolled the knell for insularity, and hence for isolationism, by striking the heart of the financial and strategic power of the United States and revealing to the American people their involvement with the darkest corners of globalization: the terrorist networks infiltrated throughout the nation, international finance and communication used for criminal purposes, the secret diplomacy linking Kabul and Islamabad to Washington. The shock of September 11 then persuaded the Americans that in the war against international terrorism that had been imposed on them they could and should count only on themselves. As we have seen, in the end the terrorist attacks deepened the incipient gulf between the United States and the rest of the world, including its European allies. The harsh initiation into international realities that the tragedy of September 11 represented for ordinary Americans was immediately coupled with a sense of ostracism or at least a lack of understanding of America, reinforcing the vicious circle of unilateralism and anti-Americanism. Finally, by directly threatening the security of the United States and its citizens in universally reprehensible terms, Al-Qaeda's declaration of war restored the national unity on foreign policy that had disappeared along with the Cold War. The isolationist logic of strict defense of the national interest, appealed to as never before in the history of the country, was reconciled with Wilsonian Messianism in defense of democratic values and world peace; the imperative of the protection of the territory and the people, with that of the preservation of collective security and Western civilization. This is why, whether the Europeans like it or not, the reorientation of foreign policy around the war against terrorism since September 11, 2001, continues to enjoy a broad consensus in the United States, and unilateralism, or more precisely, the preeminence granted to the national interest in the new American diplomacy, has every likelihood of remaining the dominant mode of projecting American power in the world for the foreseeable future.

The Ruses of Globalization

This reality does not, however, mean that Washington has by now found an adequate stance in the new international context. Quite the contrary, the new geopolitical situation has paradoxically made America diplomatically and politically more dependent on the community of nations, as illustrated by the formation of the coalition against terrorism after September 11, followed by the U.N. debate on Iraq a year later. In the view of two analysts with very different backgrounds and sensitivities, Henry Kissinger and Joseph Nye, dean of Harvard's Kennedy School of Government, the United States is still seeking a diplomacy adapted to the realities of the twenty-first century, that is, accomplishing a balanced synthesis between the strict logic of the national interest and the defense of values and the common good of the world.

According to Joseph Nye, the strategic supremacy of the United States will not be truly threatened by any other power or coalition of powers over the course of the next few decades.[3] A counteralliance bringing together Russia, China, and India is hardly likely, and Europe, potentially the most serious rival, still seems to be far from putting that primacy in peril, even if it really wanted to. But the proper use of U.S. supremacy conditions its durability in an era in which, outside the strictly military sphere, the world is already characterized more by multiple centers of power than by the monopoly that many attribute to America. In fact, while the United States enjoys unquestioned domination in the military sphere, it is not thereby in a position to impose its will in the Middle East, North Korea, or Afghanistan, contrary to conventional belief. In addition, it is subject to strong competition from Europe and Japan in the economic sphere and is seeing its advantages in the ever more essential realm of soft power eroding, as it experiences a decline in legitimacy, influence, attractiveness, and prestige within the international community.

And yet, until recently this intangible dimension was one of the

principal assets of American power, one that no other nation or civilization could aspire to rival. It resulted in fact from the combination of a reserve of sympathy arising from the accomplishments
of Wilsonian internationalism in the course of the first half of the
twentieth century, with a culture particularly in tune with modernity and universality, and political and economic strength capable
of promoting all of this in the four corners of the world. America
won the Cold War and provoked the disintegration of the Soviet
Union more through its cultural charms and its economic superiority than by means of its strategic arsenal. But the evolution of the
world over the last twenty years has contributed to the dissemination of that soft power, notably to the benefit of the unifying Europe, thereby making soft power more strategic and cutting into
the dominant position of American civilization in this domain.

Paradoxically, the first factor causing this erosion is directly
connected to the emancipatory, decentralizing, if not destabilizing,
virtues of advances in democracy and the rule of law in the international sphere, of the revolution in information and communications technologies, and, more generally, of globalization. Although these forces are still dominated by the United States to the
point of being identified by public opinion with American civilization itself, this ascendancy is destined to dwindle in time, as illustrated by the Internet, a powerful tool for the construction of an
antiestablishment "international civil society," of which the pre-
dominant language will eventually be Chinese. The conjunction of
advances in multilateralism, the information revolution, and globalization has diversified the actors on the world stage—international institutions, nongovernmental organizations, multinational
companies, terrorist networks; revalued the political, legal, and cultural instruments for exercising influence, at the expense of mere
military and economic superiority; and generally fostered the
emergence of widespread challenges to the established order, embodied by the United States alone since the victory of democracy

and capitalism over communist ideology and the positioning of Europe as the champion of soft power.

This dissemination of the new instruments of power has taken place against a background of renewed challenges to Western modernity—the consumer society, individualism, materialism, inequality; the resurgence of the confrontation between North and South; and the more or less antagonistic assertion of the diversity of identities, itself associated with the emergence of new centers of economic, political, and religious power in the developing world. Following the pattern of the demonstrations in Seattle and Florence, this "antiglobalization" protest is defined more by its worldwide extent and its ideological opposition to neoliberalism and to "imperial" America than by the coherence of its many components, giving rise to the most incongruous ties and objective alliances, in the West and elsewhere. The diffusion of access to information and technology is, moreover, at the heart of the notion of "asymmetrical threat," symbol of the circumventing of the traditional instruments of power by the destitute determined to sacrifice their own existence in order to annihilate civilian populations in defiance of any legal or moral norm, any international custom, or even any political rationale. The war declared on America by Islamism is obviously the most radical form of this challenge, but in a much more meaningful way than the traditionally ambivalent relationship between Russia or China and the United States, the emergence of almost structural conflict between Europe and America is not totally foreign to this phenomenon because it has introduced dissonance within the very heart of the Atlantic Alliance and Western civilization.

These developments, most of which have not yet produced all their effects, tend to qualify the vision of a now unipolar world and unequivocal American superiority. They portend, not the famous "American decline" dear to the hearts of European sovereignists, but the prospect of an international system traversed by economic, political, and cultural competition of varying intensity between

America and other geopolitical entities, one of the lasting lines of force in which will be anti-Americanism. The result is that the United States, however economically and militarily powerful it may be, and however universal the ideals it claims to embody and defend, cannot long prosper in a climate of hostility from the rest of the world, especially if it finds itself to be the de facto world policeman. The struggle at the United Nations over Iraq in the fall of 2002 and thereafter showed that the perpetuation of this kind of antagonism, or of coalitions founded purely on the convergence of interests rather than on shared values and a common fate, would in the long run weaken America and the Western camp and at the very least strengthen Washington's unilateralist tendencies. The issue of the legitimacy, or more precisely, as the term implies no value judgment, of the acceptability, of external action by the United States in the eyes of the international community has thus become critical as much for the stability of the world as for the United States itself.

The Price of Exceptionalism

The answer to this question, if the aim is greater international openness in American diplomacy, cannot come from a simplistic denunciation of unilateralism or from more or less well intentioned European critical inclinations toward one or another aspect of the "American model." It will come even less from language explicitly or implicitly justifying the terror of September 11 by the misdeeds of American foreign policy and the wrongs of the West throughout the world; morally unacceptable and intellectually erroneous, this argument is rightly seen as inadmissible by the United States.

Bringing America and the other actors of the international community closer together requires in reality neither compromise with nor accommodation to terrorism and other declared or potential threats to the security of the United States, its allies, or the rest of the world. As we have seen, it is not entirely a matter of American responsibility either, because Washington's unilateralism is structurally linked to the diplomatic and strategic absence of Europe. Criticism of current American foreign policy calls, therefore, for the Europeans to deal with their own problems first by asserting themselves as a responsible interlocutor for Washington and for the rest of the world. But America must of course do its part by bringing its foreign policy into harmony with its status as the sole superpower and with the evolution of the international system. If the rationale for American exceptionalism is understandable, this attitude is nonetheless increasingly out of tune with what has become, for the better, the dominant culture of that system. In fact international relations depend ever more on a network of institutions, norms, and procedures intended to assure the dominance of the rule of law, dialogue, negotiation, and solidarity over relationships of force within the community of nations. Legalistic multilateralism thus represents the new institutional language, and it will continue to spread along with the globalization of problems and of the collective and negotiated solutions needed to address them. For the United States, this is one of the principal challenges of globalization, which to other eyes still seems to be a simple export of American neoliberalism.

Current American prejudices against multilateralism are all the more paradoxical because America invented and promoted this doctrine around the world. Universal values, collective security, international institutions, and humanitarian law were in fact directly derived from Wilsonian idealism, as was the League of Nations, the precursor of the United Nations. The United States was also, as early as 1944, behind the various institutions set up at Bretton Woods—GATT, the IMF, the World Bank—which still handle issues relating to trade, development, and the regulation of the world economy and financial markets. It was the United States as well that fostered the establishment and growth of the European Community, inspired the creation of the OECD and the G7, and sponsored the Conference on Security and Cooperation in Europe (CSCE), the Final Act of which served as a decisive ideological

weapon against totalitarianism in Central and Eastern Europe from
the mid-1970s on. More profoundly, the idea of replacing relations
of force with collective negotiations on the basis of a set of rules
of law, institutions, and procedures derives directly from the constitutional heritage of the greatest democracy in the world.

Under American influence, the two world wars led the international community, notably the Europeans, who were particularly
lacking in this area, to articulate and constitutionalize fundamental rights by entrusting jurisdictional supervision of them to national supreme courts or their equivalents. For Europe as a whole,
the European Convention for the Protection of Human Rights,
adopted in 1950, played a major role in promoting the rule of law
in Western Europe, and later in the eastern half of the Continent.
In the course of the 1990s the European Union itself moved into
the field of fundamental rights and, in the preambles to the Maastricht and Amsterdam treaties and then in the European Charter
of Fundamental Rights, adopted in Nice in December 2000, made
it one of the pillars of its political identity. How, then, are we to explain that while this legalistic and multilateralist culture was gradually becoming the common norm, the United States was moving
further and further away from it, as a now irritating legacy?

The fact is that unlike Europe, America has never really had to
confront the question of a partial renunciation of its own absolute
national sovereignty. In the isolationist tradition, foreign policy was
supposed to be confined to providing a virtuous example by per-
fecting domestic democracy and avoiding foreign entanglements.
The Wilsonian diplomacy of the twentieth century, of course,
broke with this minimalist vision by shaping the international system in the image of American democracy, but it never gave up any
fraction of national sovereignty. On the contrary, the United States
has always taken great care not to hinder its freedom of movement
by restrictive commitments, and the two-thirds Senate majority required for ratification of international treaties serves as a particularly effective protection in this regard. Similarly, the United States

has always dominated international organizations, or at least held a right of veto over their decisions. Seen in this historical perspective, the current conflict between American unilateralism and the multilateralism of the rest of the world is primarily a reflection of the divergent development of the protagonists. As it has become increasingly democratic, the international community has turned into a vast network of institutions and principles in which America is a full participant because of globalization. But at the same time, the United States has considerably increased its power and autonomy and become less inclined to bow to new multilateral constraints because they are generally in the hands of institutions that have grown bureaucratic and governments that assert their rebellion or hostility to its values and its foreign policy. With isolationism no longer possible, unilateralism seems to be the natural result of the conjunction of compelled internationalism with an exacerbated sense of national sovereignty.

This dynamic comes on top of America's longstanding suspicion of the cowardly, futile, and in the end murderous compromises with the enemy embodied in the collective unconscious by the appeasement policy of Daladier and Chamberlain at Munich, which were responsible for allowing Hitler to invade Czechoslovakia in 1938 in the hope of limiting Nazi expansion at that point. In recent years that suspicion of the scraps of paper of international legality has been bolstered in American public opinion by Iraq's continuing violation of U.N. resolutions, by the torpedoing of the Oslo peace process between Israel and the Palestinians by extremists on both sides, and by North Korea's breach of the 1994 antinuclear pact with the United States. These experiences have reinforced the idea that international institutions and treaties have as their principal result the protection of treaty violations by "rogue" states while constraining the freedom of action of the international community, including in respect of the threat of force, whose effectiveness America has frequently experienced, notably against the Soviet Union.

What is the way out of this deadlock? The debate on American unilateralism is not dissimilar to the familiar confrontation between sovereignists and federalists in Europe. America and the international community now find themselves in an opposition analogous to the one that has existed for fifty years between national sovereignty and European integration. Like London confronting Brussels, Washington seems to cling to complete autonomy in defiance of the constraints of political globalization. The parallel has its limits, of course: however constraining it may be in fact, globalization cannot be assimilated to the extremely elaborate and freely agreed upon political project of European unification. Even in the economic realm, the European Community has no equivalent on a world scale. In addition, and most importantly, the principal justification in the view of member states and of public opinion for the abandonment or sharing of sovereignty required by European unification has revolved around the de facto erosion of the prerogatives of nation-states exposed to the strong winds of globalization, a reasoning successfully articulated by the advocates of the euro. The argument obviously does not work for the American superpower, which the EU is intended precisely to counterbalance. Quite the contrary, for the United States, the existence of its power and autonomy, as well as its unshakeable faith in the universality of its democratic values, constitutes now more than ever the principal force behind its assertion of national sovereignty.

Despite these differences, consideration of the limits of national sovereignty in a globalized world probably provide the best hope for an eventual shrinking of the ideological gap between the United States and the rest of the world, particularly Europe, in this respect. From the American point of view, the justification for a more multilateral approach to international relations would thus be based not so much on the loss of sovereignty engendered by globalization (although that argument retains its relevance) as on the position of world leadership imposed on America by its status as the only superpower, by the responsibility it therefore has toward the international community, and finally by the consensual approach required in order to grant U.S. foreign policy legitimacy and effectiveness.

In the late 1980s, in the context of the debate over further European economic and monetary integration, a French expert report tried to evaluate the "cost of a non-Europe," that is, the losses and the risks that would be incurred by the European economy in the event that national regulatory and currency differences were maintained. The analysis encouraged the advent of the single market on January 1, 1993, and the introduction of the euro a few years later. A similar exercise addressing American exceptionalism and unilateralism, although more difficult to carry out on such an intangible question, would presumably produce a similar awareness and greater openness to the outside world on the part of fortress America. Beyond hostility, the global cost of American exceptionalism is measured in a significant loss of legitimacy, aura, and influence, notably in the view of the most traditional U.S. allies, such as Germany, Turkey, the moderate Arab countries, and even Japan.[4] This loss, even distrust, now operates as a political brake on Washington's freedom of movement on the international stage, despite the lever that the global war against terrorism provides to American diplomacy. Moreover, the decline in the international influence of the United States is not limited to foreign policy and security but reaches, much more diffusely, into the sphere of the economy and trade, where Europe is of almost equal weight, and even more paradoxically, into the ethical and cultural realm, where America's exemplary character is increasingly overshadowed by parochialism or even archaism.

As an illustration, if there is one area, both legal and cultural, in which the international influence of Europe now surpasses that of the United States, it is the realm, highly emblematic of the American democratic ideal, of human rights. This is only an apparent paradox. Europe in fact had two major advantages over the United States in the process of constitutionalization and internationalization of human rights that gradually spread throughout the democratic world after 1945. The first was a result of Europe's relatively recent conversion, compared with that of America, to an operational, not merely philosophical and political, conception of human rights. This time lag enabled the Old Continent to integrate into its conception of human rights the main advances of the twentieth century, notably in economic and social matters, particularly relevant to the developing world. Europe's second advantage was linked to its universalist tradition, given substance by the experience of intra-European dialogue involved in building the European Community itself. Hence, more modern and more universal than the decisions of the U.S. Supreme Court—which are dependent on the particularities or even archaisms of American federalism and on the politically charged character of questions that are matters of consensus in Europe, such as abortion and the death penalty—those of the European Court of Human Rights and the constitutional courts around the continent have become ever more frequent precedents for the supreme courts of South Africa, Argentina, India, and even Canada.

The relative marginalization of the United States in the process of developing a universal law of human rights, a reflection of the voluntary or compelled isolationism of the U.S. Supreme Court, is also a product of American schizophrenia with respect to international norms. Whereas the promotion of human rights around the world has generally been pursued by Democratic administrations, the reluctance of the Senate to ratify international conventions, including humanitarian conventions, has also been constant. Moreover, unlike the situation in Europe and in many non-European countries, American law grants to international treaties only relative legal primacy over domestic law—that is, a primacy always subject to reversal by the passage of a subsequent contradictory law—which underlines the particularism and reduces the international normative influence of the United States outside the economic sphere. Conversely, thanks to a policy of actively promoting international conventions and clearly recognizing their primacy over domestic law, Europe now occupies a much more central role in the development of a global legal order.

Toward a New Leadership

More convincing than many groundless accusations, awareness of the costs of its exceptionalism should encourage the United States to rethink its relationship with the rest of the world. Its prestige has never been greater than when it generously shared its prosperity, its power, and its ideals with others, that is, in the era of reconstruction and creativity following the defeat of Nazism. The war that radical Islamism has declared against the entire civilized world has perhaps offered the United States the opportunity to reformulate the synthesis that legitimated its diplomacy over the course of most of the twentieth century by transcending current unilateralism with a new internationalism. If, as is unfortunately likely, the fight against hyperterrorism has to remain a lasting focus of American foreign policy, this orientation will require the continuing cooperation of the international community, and reciprocally, will work to benefit the entire world. The United States therefore has every interest in changing the way it looks at the rest of the world so that it no longer sees multilateralism as a constraint imposed on its sovereignty but rather as an opportunity for the conscious exercise of a leadership that the majority of nations call for. Despite the Bush administration's unilateralist rhetoric since September 11, its general attitude, from the diplomatic efforts of Colin Powell to the pronounced Wilsonian flavor of some of the president's speeches and strategic initiatives, has pointed in that direction.[5]

This search for a new internationalism will no doubt require a reexamination of the place of foreign affairs in the political life and the institutional system of the United States. The conjunction of superpower status with globalization in fact requires a change in the historical hierarchy between domestic and foreign policy. Foreign policy is still too marginal and often subordinate to powerful special interests, and the shaping of domestic policy is unconcerned with the increasing permeability in all fields of activity; a better balance between the demands of both is necessary. One should not, however, underestimate how difficult it is for a nation the size of the United States to carry out such a change, given its strong isolationist tradition and the unexampled complexity of its political processes and internal contradictions. The challenge is principally a cultural one, involving America' self-image as *primus inter pares* in a world society governed by rules and as a republic that is both "imperial" and exceptional.

As the world's greatest power, although it has no colonialist past and is lacking in the hegemonic or imperialist aims often attributed to it, the United States must begin to listen to the world, something it seems to find increasingly difficult to do, even in the case of its European allies. In this regard, power, dynamism, and prosperity turn out to be formidable handicaps. Americans often feel that they can accomplish and know everything by themselves, that the contributions of others are of no use to them. This is the case in military affairs, but the same attitude can be seen in economic, scientific, and cultural life. The United States is convinced not only that it has the best hospitals and universities and the best-endowed museums and libraries, the best bankers and lawyers and the greatest scientists, but also that it is the most cosmopolitan society in the world because of its liberal immigration policy and the openness of its universities, laboratories, and think tanks to the intellectual elite of the entire world.

Since diplomacy is also a matter of psychology, the fact that all this is largely true does not lessen the arrogance the rest of the world sees in this attitude nor the resulting resentment. Furthermore, American superiority in the realm of knowledge in the broadest sense does not guarantee real familiarity with the diversity and complexity of the world, because the multiculturalist prism through which the United States views those factors is largely shaped by American political, social, intellectual, and of course commercial norms. On the contrary, the fact that the U.S. domestic market is closed to large areas of world scholarly, literary, and artistic production not in tune with those norms and that international news, notably European politics, occupies a marginal place in the U.S. media has strongly contributed to the increasing international ignorance and insularity of American society. This ignorance, however, is entirely reciprocal, since fascination with and hostility toward the United States abroad are generally based solely on the most superficial contacts with a particularly diverse and ever more singular nation. Finally, American self-satisfaction has increasingly shown its limitations, even measured against its own scale of values, whether in the failures of business regulation illustrated by the accounting and financial scandals of Enron and WorldCom or in the intelligence failures revealed by the September 11 attacks. These difficulties have legitimated the self-assertiveness of the rest of the world, notably Europe, in the face of an arrogance that has been assimilated to the very identity of the United States.

Were the United States to achieve this kind of awareness, the first institutional consequence should be a greatly increased emphasis on the nonmilitary components of its external activities, notably diplomacy, intelligence, international cooperation, public development aid, and cultural affairs. The State Department budget now represents only 1 percent of the national budget (compared with 4 percent in the 1960s), whereas 16 percent is devoted to defense.[6] In qualitative terms, the restoration of a highly qualified foreign service must also remedy the unfortunate tendency to distribute ambassadorships, including the most strategic ones, to large contributors to presidential campaigns. The objective should be to reoccupy the multilateral field and to commit to the role of leader of the international community, beyond that of world policeman and recalcitrant supplier of funds to international organizations. The payment of back dues to the United Nations and the return to the United Nations Educational, Scientific, and Cultural Organization (UNESCO), boycotted since 1984, represent a first step in this direction. The global and multifarious character of the war against international terrorism should, further, bring the United States to redefine its attitude to the developing world and to the major global issues and to encourage the democratization of the Arab world and its integration into the world economy. This twofold task obviously requires the active participation of the international community, Europe in particular. But it cannot occur without America's constructive involvement in Africa and the Arab-Muslim world, analogous to its postwar role in Europe and as leader of the free world.

Of course, times have changed, and the United States now considers itself to be at war, while at the same time seeing itself as the only true guardian of world peace. Its commitment to multilateralism hence probably requires others to make some accommodations in those areas—which are fewer and fewer—that lack a body of international rules and in circumstances where multilateral procedures produce results in direct conflict with America's national interest or that of its allies. Finally, and most importantly, the return of the United States to a more consensual diplomacy presupposes that all members of the international community, including non-Western nations, confirm their support for the principles, norms, and values that are the basis of the international system and accept their universality without qualification.

This prospect may seem utopian in light of the current state of world affairs, American political life, and the hardly Rooseveltian spirit that now prevails in Washington. But just as Europe is compelled to carry out major political and strategic changes if it wants to make a difference on the international stage, does the United States have any other way to legitimate its supremacy and to carry out in depth the battle of the civilized world against the terrorist threat, the forces that nourish it, and the pretexts that it uses than to reinvent an internationalist diplomacy uniting leadership and generosity under the banners of Omaha Beach, Bretton Woods, and Camp David?

Chapter 6

FOR A NEW ALLIANCE

What will transatlantic relations look like twenty, thirty, or fifty years from now? Will the present distance between the United States and Europe be long-lasting, or is it a transitory ordeal or even a mere episode in a complex and shifting history? Is it reversible, or will it intensify and lead to divorce? The answers to these difficult questions, essential for our future and that of the international system, are far from clear-cut.

According to one point of view, imperturbably serene and corresponding to longstanding official discourse on both sides of the Atlantic, the tensions of recent years have had no serious effects on Atlantic solidarity, which is based not only on a community of values but also on the economic interdependence embodied in $2 trillion of annual trade and investment. These are passing frictions, coming after many others in the history of transatlantic relations, and they will be resolved in time, with changing circumstances and the expression of a little mutual goodwill. At the other extreme, the alarmist position, based largely on reciprocal demonization, foresees the gradual transformation of the alliance into antagonism. Some American neoconservatives are dismissing the Old Continent as irrelevant, while others are worried about the growing

power of a Europe perceived as increasingly opposed to the United
States, indirectly inducing hostility to the progress of European political integration. Conversely, in Europe the anti-American lobby
has taken advantage of current divergences to proclaim the un-
avoidable divorce between a Europe in the process of emancipating
itself and an America that has become dangerously uncontrollable
in the face of its allegedly coming decline.[1]

As usual, the truth lies somewhere in between. Even if it is essentially accurate, the official discourse sidesteps the set of centrifugal forces described in the preceding chapters and their impact
on transatlantic relations in the long run. This diplomatic language
is thus partially obsolete and counterproductive because it avoids
any analysis of the factors causing estrangement and ways of dealing with them, in the same fashion as the recurring denial in official rhetoric on both sides of the Rhine of the estrangement between France and Germany at work since the end of the Cold War.
As for the alarmist and antagonistic discourse, it is obviously questionable because it is generally inspired by archaic reciprocal prejudices. Bolstered by the media's natural failing of exaggeration, it
tends to blow any transatlantic difference out of proportion in
order to support its position.

Scenarios for Tomorrow

Between the soothing wishful thinking of the Atlanticists and the
separatist ulterior motives of the opponents of the Alliance there is
room for genuine concern about the capacity of the United States
and Europe to preserve for the long term a solidarity whose renewed necessity I have attempted to demonstrate. It is true that
transatlantic ties remain solid and can still be restored and
strengthened, but this will not occur without real efforts on both
sides aimed at counteracting the many factors working in the opposite direction. The American side clearly has the easier task. In
essence, it is up to the United States to fully assume its role as consensual and legitimate leader of the international community, to

commit itself more actively and generously to the resolution of major world problems, and to take pains to maintain a privileged relation with the European Union. For the principal strategic and economic power in the world this involves above all diplomacy and leadership, that is, political wisdom. It is therefore reasonable to hope that succeeding American administrations will be able to understand the importance of this course of conduct, as much for the United States as for Atlantic relations and world stability, and put it into practice. Despite the criticisms directed against it and its unquestionably blundering style, the Bush administration has already begun the transition from the blunt unilateralism of its first year in power toward a new internationalism, to be sure "distinctively American," as President Bush characterized it, but one that the international community as a whole may be able to accept. Reengagement with the United Nations and the prewar efforts to reach a consensus on Iraqi disarmament in the Security Council, albeit unsuccessful, were steps in the right direction.

For Europe the challenge is of another order of difficulty, if one recognizes that bridging the present Atlantic divide is dependent upon reducing the strategic and diplomatic imbalance that prevails between the two partners of the alliance. Past experience induces great skepticism about the EU's capacity, especially after its enlargement to twenty-five members, to mobilize the political consensus and the financial resources required to accede to the position of a significant player on the world stage. If the status quo prevails, European dependence on America and the new-style NATO will de facto continue, and the transatlantic relationship will pursue its long and tumultuous course. This is the choice of the Atlanticists in both Washington and the European capitals, and a very realistic hypothesis.

However, the ability of an economic and political entity with a population of more than 450 million to remain for long a political and military dwarf in the international system of the twenty-first century appears highly questionable. This leads just as reasonably

to the opposite hypothesis, according to which in one way or another, through the European Union itself or through an institutionalized subgroup of member states, or even by a simple mandate
conferred on one country or a group of countries, depending on
the circumstances—as was, for example, implicitly the case with
France in the U.N. negotiations on Iraq in the fall of 2002—Europe will eventually become a more consistent diplomatic and
strategic interlocutor for the United States. After all, the fact that
it has been possible to make the European Union as such one of
the protagonists of this book is an encouraging sign of the existence, embryonic as it may be, of a common strategic vision for Europeans.

If this second requirement for strengthening transatlantic ties is
one day fulfilled, the question will finally arise of the proper positioning of a Europe that has become an actor on the world political stage vis-à-vis the American superpower. This question has to
be addressed now, not only because it is the keystone of a rebuilding of the Alliance on new foundations but also because within the
Union it is a precondition for the very possibility of the rise of European power, along with the encouragement that the United
States might usefully provide, as it did after 1945, to this final stage
in the political unification of the continent. Even if they generally
remain skeptical about the capacity of Europeans to rise to the
challenge, American foreign-policy experts include many advocates
for a strengthening of Europe, rightly convinced that a political
and strategic readjustment between the two sides of the Atlantic
would be a blessing for the United States itself as well as for Atlantic relations and for the rest of the world.[2] But against this Eu-
rophile party stands the camp of those who have always been suspicious of European integration and who have seen their fears
confirmed in the last few years and months by the coincidence of
the affirmation of European identity on the international stage with
the emergence of a structural antagonism toward the United States
in the European discourse.[3] After the transatlantic tension over

Iraq, the supporters of this view, neoconservatives who are now very influential in Washington, have every reason to oppose an increase in the power of the EU, perceived as contrary to American interests and corrosive to transatlantic solidarity. Accordingly, establishing stronger and better ties between the American superpower and the political Europe in formation requires, today more than ever, that the latter stop looking for the glue holding it together in a systematic opposition to the United States and instead think of itself as powerful and different *alongside* the United States.

One should not underestimate the difficulty of adopting such a position on the part of a political entity still in search of its identifying features and conceived in constant reference to the United States, going so far as to consider calling itself "United States of Europe," a phrase dating back to the federalist utopian perspective of the 1950s, recently reactivated by President Giscard d'Estaing in the context of the Convention on the Future of Europe. The relationship to America, which in the interim has become the only global power, has thus taken on a quasi-ontological dimension for Europe, and the tendency toward differentiation, if not opposition, has become a natural reflex for an entity in search of existence in the shadow of American hegemony, an entity that in addition bears its own, more broadly consensual vision of the international system. The difficulty of defining a European identity in the context of globalization and enlargement of the EU, as well as the weakness or even the absence of Europe on the international stage, fosters, as we have seen, the systematic tendency to give prominence to differences, defensive attitudes, and irresponsibility. Washington's indifference to international pressures concerning the Kyoto Protocol and the treaty establishing the International Criminal Court thus led Europe to mobilize the rest of the planet against American positions and in favor of their ratification. Differentiation, critical distance, and even opposition vis-à-vis the United States are thus inherent in the process of establishing of European political identity and its affirmation on the world stage. But that attitude should be articulated, particularly in addressing public opinion, as a contribution to the Atlantic partnership in the framework of fundamental solidarity with the United States rather than as the levers of a planetary rivalry with it.

There are good reasons for hoping that this change of attitude will eventually occur naturally, power bringing with it responsibility, and the rebalancing of forces producing the need for cooperation and compromise. The relationship between Europe and America indeed never functions as well as when Europe finds itself on a more or less equal footing with the United States. This is the case in the area of economic regulation, both in competition policy, where Washington and Brussels cooperate harmoniously, and in international trade policy, where disputes do not in any way call into question the adherence of the two parties to a common body of principles and rules or their cooperation in multilateral negotiations.

The Forest and the Trees

In fact, the principal threat to transatlantic solidarity lies in the insidious indoctrination of public opinion by politicians and the media in favor of the separatist argument. Differences of course exist, and they will likely intensify as a result of demographic, social, cultural, and strategic developments at work on both sides of the Atlantic. But this reality makes it all the more incumbent on Europeans and Americans to fight against the estrangement whose seeds it carries by rediscovering the abandoned paths of dialogue and mutual understanding instead of confining themselves to compiling an inventory of arbitrarily combined areas of disagreement. To that extent, prevailing media discourse on the transatlantic divide fosters the reality that it denounces insofar as it does not bring with it a critical and constructive reflection on the nature of the problem and ways to resolve it.

The first antidote to this drift consists in not missing the forest for the trees. Just as trade disputes are only a few drops of water in the ocean of transatlantic economic interdependence, so cultural and philosophical differences over a few powerfully symbolic subjects, such as the death penalty and human rights, seem to be not only exaggerated but in fact marginal in the context of the convergence process that has characterized the development of economies, societies, and ways of living in the New World and the Old since 1945.

Within the Western world, the major historical development of the last half-century has indeed been the convergence of the European and American models around the now shared norms of the market economy, free trade, political freedoms, and regulation through law, under the influence of the opening of borders, of European unification, and of the ideological triumph of liberalism over Marxism and communism. As a practical matter this means that the economies and the democracies of Europe and the United States now function along comparable lines; that on either side of the Atlantic businessmen, lawyers, and journalists now speak the same language; that societies are much more transparent to one another even in their particularities.

One might object that this convergence is essentially the product of the Americanization of the world, of the conversion of Europe, like other regions of the planet, to the essential values of the American system, in the economic as well as the political and cultural realms, and that this conversion has been accomplished under the influence of ideological, institutional, and economic mediations that are now vigorously challenged, such as neoliberalism, globalization, or European integration. However pertinent it might be, the objection nevertheless omits the freely accepted and very broadly positive character throughout Europe of the transformation of closed and administered economies into open and competitive markets, of authoritarian or Jacobin regimes into constitutional and pluralist democracies, of monolithic and conservative societies into pluralistic communities increasingly governed by the rule of law. It also forgets that the bases of political and economic liberalism were established in Europe in the seventeenth and-

eighteenth centuries, before they came into conflict with the iner-
tia of the *ancien régime* and the ideologies of revolution, Jacobin-
ism, and collectivism. Thus, the Americanization that is so often
incriminated is also a return to the ideas exiled for two centuries by
the vicissitudes of European political history. The reintroduction
into Europe of ideas and practices first experienced in the United
States can also produce reciprocal effects in their country of origin. On the world stage Europe has, for example, become the
champion of a legalistic and multilateralist view of international relations initially derived from Wilsonian idealism but now mark-
ing its distinction from American unilateralism. Here too the transition toward a genuine cross-fertilization of models between the
United States and Europe depends essentially on the capacity of
the latter to increase its international normative influence, which
is in turn a function of the more or less exclusive character of EU
jurisdiction and the more or less uniform character of European
legal norms in the area concerned. The European Union can already lay claim to remarkable accomplishments in this respect in
matters of economic and trade regulation, and it is reasonable to
anticipate the advent of a more balanced convergence between the
two principal poles of the Western world within a matter of years.[4]

In the contested domain of foreign policy the consensus of public opinion on the two continents is greater than can be inferred
from official positions and media pronouncements. According to
the largest opinion poll ever carried out in the Atlantic Alliance,
published in September 2002 by the Chicago Council on Foreign
Relations and the German Marshall Fund of the United States,
Americans and Europeans still share the same values, the same view
of the world, and the same fears, and they still consider each other
solid allies.[5] A vast majority of Americans favored strong U.S. involvement in the world, preferably within the framework of the
United Nations and with the support of the international community, and deplored the unilateralism of the Bush administration on
the Kyoto Protocol and the International Criminal Court. Con-

versely, most Europeans expressed strong sympathy for the U.S. war on international terrorism and even for America's determination to disarm Iraq. They declared themselves prepared to see Europe assume responsibilities as a "superpower" alongside the United States and to resort to force if necessary. The principal differences between American and European attitudes amounted to a less favorable opinion in Europe of the Bush administration's foreign policy and to the understandable wish on the part of the Americans to maintain their status as the only superpower. This diagnosis was confirmed as of December 2002 by the worldwide poll of the Pew Research Center, directed by Madeleine Albright, according to which the image of the United States remains very positive in European countries (with more than 60 percent of opinions favorable), unlike the situation prevailing among America's non-Western allies. This comforting evidence of the solidity of the alliance among its vital elements is an encouragement to combat the centrifugal forces at work and the separatist strategies advocated by certain media outlets, ideologists, and governments.

Even with respect to the conflict in the Middle East the traditional divergence between the two sides of the Atlantic seems to result principally from different evaluations of the balance of forces. For the United States, the survival and security of Israel are by no means assured, and they constitute, in addition to a moral obligation, a strategic imperative for national and Western interests. Generally hostile to the use of force, Europe, for its part, manifestly underestimates the vulnerability of the Jewish state but professes the same attachment as the United States to its security. Here too there should thus be a basis for a convergence of points of view, if not of diplomatic stances.

A Clash of Civilizations?

Having ensured that the tree of discord does not make one lose sight of the forest of transatlantic convergence, let us consider what is apparently the most sensitive branch of that tree, namely, the

conflict of values, if not of civilizations, which according to some
is carrying Europeans and Americans further apart every day. This
alleged ideological divide is said to be evident on questions as essential as the two societies' relationship to nature (the debates on
climate change, sustainable development, genetically modified organisms), to the rule of law (international treaties, the International
Criminal Court), to man and society (the death penalty, human
rights, criminal justice), and even to the divine (through the influence of religion and moralism on society and government). On all
these major questions it is as though the political and cultural split
had taken precedence over economic convergence, in transatlantic
relations as well as around the world.

Let us point at the outset to an obvious fact: these areas of an alleged clash of civilizations between Europe and the United States
go back to the stereotypes of the most archaic anti-Americanism,
that of eighteenth-century France, which saw Americans as the
barbarians of the New World.[6] According to that view, while postwar Europe was ascending the ladder of civilization, the most sophisticated modernity had not succeeded in eradicating the
primeval barbarism of America: violence, disrespect for the law,
manipulation of nature, fundamentalism. Reality, however, turns
out to be quite different for anyone who cares to reject hasty assimilation of disparate phenomena and to treat each situation on
its own terms and merits.

Let us begin with "nature." The American rejection of the now
famous Kyoto Protocol, which the Europeans took five years to
ratify, has little to do with contempt for the environment or with
any "philosophy." In the context of scientific uncertainty about the
precise effects of climate change it reflected the concern to preserve
American industry from constraints that were considered excessive
and from which the largest polluters of the developing world were
exempt. Since then the United States has put in place a national
program of voluntary reduction of greenhouse gas emissions,
which is less penalizing for U.S. growth, on which the world econ-

omy continues to depend. Considerable sums have been invested on this basis in technological and industrial research in the United States, while the European countries may prove unable to meet their Kyoto commitments.[7]

Another sensitive matter, the issue of genetically modified organisms, or GMOs, inextricably mixes concerns with public health and the environment, cultural considerations about the relationship to food, and most of all substantial industrial and commercial interests. The United States has for a long time been producing food containing GMOs. In June 1999 the European Union decreed a moratorium on such production in the name of precaution in order to provide time for the adoption of a regulatory scheme for consumer protection. With this scheme now complete, and in the absence of scientific evidence attesting to the harmfulness of food containing GMOs, the industrial and commercial dimension of the debate will come to the fore, within the EU as well as in the World Trade Organization, where Europe has already lost the battle of the ban on hormone-treated beef. Once again, two attitudes toward scientific and technical risk may be contrasted, but above all, formidable economic and commercial interests and important development issues are at stake. In this instance as well, Europe, whose principal spokesman seems to be the French antiglobalization propagandist José Bové, risks remaining largely on the sidelines of the biotechnology revolution if it does not soon climb aboard the moving train.

Let us now turn to the accusation of contempt for international law and justice. The Bush administration did indeed make the mistake of bluntly rejecting a series of international treaties, almost all of which had not yet been signed or ratified, when it came to power. It may also be criticized for its total indifference to justifying its positions on the matter in the eyes of the world. But those justifications nonetheless exist in the light of the national interest of the United States, its global responsibilities, and the very credibility of international law, particularly concerning certain treaties negotiated in haste. The validity of American positions must, therefore, be considered on a case-by-case basis. As an illustration, the rejection by the Clinton administration of the treaty on antipersonnel mines was not an expression of enthusiasm for that type of weapon; rather it was aimed, in the absence of a specific exemption, at protecting American forces stationed in South Korea, whose security depends on those mines. The refusal of the United States to participate in the International Criminal Court is more controversial because international criminal justice represents an essential victory of the rule of law over the *raison d'état*. But this victory is recent and revolutionary in light of the international legal tradition of the Western world. In this context, the failure to submit to Congress the 1998 treaty signed by Bill Clinton is not meant to express any complacency toward dictatorships or crimes against humanity; rather it is intended to protect members of the U.S. armed forces engaged in peacekeeping operations in the four corners of the world against unfounded accusations motivated by essentially political considerations. This suspicion may be considered excessive, but it is not incomprehensible in these times of global anti-Americanism and worldwide engagement by the United States. Generally speaking, although the American stance toward certain treaties may be considered selfish and unilateralistic, it does not reflect a conflict of values on any subject whatever, including respect for international law, but rather a sovereign judgment, broadly bipartisan, about the interests of America in the light of its global strategic and economic responsibilities.[8] Besides, it is likely that a little more diplomacy on both sides would have made American participation in many of these treaties possible, at the price of a few modifications or exemptions.

The analysis is not very different when it comes to the way in which the United States is conducting the war against terrorism, whether we consider the "unconventional" treatment of prisoners in Guantanamo or the unduly emphasized theory of "preemption," under which America has claimed the right to make preventive strikes against targets that constitute a genuine, serious and permanent threat to its security or to that of its allies and the rest of the world. From the U.S. point of view, terrorism should not be governed by the laws of war and conventional strategy, because it infringes on their most fundamental principles. As for "preemptive war," this is less a matter of a revolutionary strategic doctrine in the history of international relations than one of a shift based on common sense in the current context. Once again, and even though it is the party principally concerned, Washington deserves the reproach of unilateralism on these strategic and legal questions that concern the international community as a whole. But while U.S. positions are a legitimate matter for debate, they do not provide any further support for the thesis of a transatlantic clash of civilizations. It is even reasonable to assume that if Europe were a superpower and the principal target of Islamist terrorism, it would adopt positions on these questions similar to those of the United States.

Finally, let us consider the only truly ethical question that separates Europe and America: the use of the death penalty. In this area Europe can take pride in having banned the use of capital punishment through the European Convention for the Protection of Human Rights and then made that prohibition one of the basic elements of its political and moral identity. All the member states of the European Union have abolished the death penalty in their national legislation, and they have consecrated respect for human life in the European Charter of Fundamental Rights, adopted in Nice in December 2000. This stand is now one of the distinctive characteristics of Europe vis-à-vis the rest of the world and the symbol of its commitment at the forefront of the fight for human rights. In contrast, the United States has yet to declare capital punishment to be unconstitutional, and as a result a minority of American states, mainly in the South, share that practice with America's worst enemies, to the chagrin of U.S. and international human-rights organizations. At a time when Western economic and

democratic cultures are converging, this anomaly is deeply shocking to the European conscience, and for the last few years human-
rights activists have made it one of their chief targets. As the Europeans often fail to realize, however, the subject is not amenable
to diplomatic pressure insofar as neither the administration nor
Congress has the slightest power to force Texas, Virginia, or Al-
abama to abolish capital punishment. Only the Supreme Court is
in a position to do so by declaring the death penalty contrary to the
American conception of human rights, but it has always refused to
do so on those terms, choosing rather to restrict the conditions for
its application.

The question is, then, whether this indisputable difference between Europe and the United States, which is bound up with the
history of the American nation and the political structures of federalism, deserves to be elevated to the rank of cultural and ethical
casus belli between the two side of the Atlantic or should rather
be taken for what it is, namely, a regrettable archaism that is a product of the sovereignty of American states, over which neither Europe nor even the U.S. federal government has any control. In support of this view, it is worth noting that capital punishment is
frequent in only a minority of states, that large segments of the
American public have reservations about it, and, more generally,
that there are throughout the world irreducible cultural particularities that it is not always the purpose of diplomacy to eliminate.
Moreover, it is not impossible that the continued pressure of international public opinion and the difficulties the use of the death
penalty engenders for international cooperation in matters of criminal justice may lead to a change in the Supreme Court's position
or even the position of some states on the question. But however
disturbing it may be, the existence of the death penalty cannot seriously be used as a justification for characterizing the United
States as a barbaric nation disrespectful of human rights nor to sub-
stantiate the argument of an ethical gulf between the two sides of
the Atlantic.

The wide dissemination of firearms and its effect on the level of criminal violence in American society, as well as the greater influence of religion and morality on American than on European public life, are elements in the same cultural constellation, although they do not involve the political and ethical concerns raised by the death penalty. The complexity of the first question, which is principally a matter of American domestic politics (although the National Rifle Association was able to prevent ratification of the treaty restricting the distribution of small arms), is illustrated with intelligence and humor in Michael Moore's recent film *Bowling for Columbine*. It turns out that Canadians are as fond of firearms as their southern neighbors, although they do not suffer from high levels of criminal violence, nor are they subject to attack for "cultural deviance" by the Europeans. As for the traditional religiosity and moralism of American society, to which many Europeans seem to be awaking, they have never called into question the attachment of the oldest modern democracy to the principles of secularism and the separation of church and state. Christian fundamentalism does influence the right wing of the Republican Party, but the claim of its influence on the Bush administration is highly controversial. The United States is the country with the greatest religious diversity in the world, at a time when Turkey's candidacy for membership and the prospect of a constitution have begun to force the European Union to confront its own identity in this area.[9]

For a Euro-Atlanticism

This brief survey of matters in dispute between Europe and the United States confirms that the real threat weighing on transatlantic relations today is found less in the intensity and the impact of divergences between societies, however real they may be, than in the use made of them in addressing public opinion, because of intellectual laziness, media bias, or political calculation. Separatist strategies are strongly fostered by the disconnection between certain underlying developments on both sides of the Atlantic and even more by the striking impoverishment of dialogue outside the economic sphere and diplomatic circles.

It thus appears urgent to rediscover the spirit of postwar mutual trust and cooperation, among governments as well as in political and intellectual circles, with a view to defusing false disputes and taking on the real factors of estrangement, whether they are structural or simply psychological. The return of liberalism to the lands of its origin should facilitate a more intimate dialogue between European and American intellectuals. With respect to governments, regular political and strategic coordination should be institutionalized between the United States and the European Union, outside the framework of NATO and the G8 summits, once the EU has adopted an appropriate representative and decision-making structure. As far as civil society is concerned, the post-Enron challenge to the supremacy of the marketplace should encourage the globalized elites of Europe and America to renew their interest in the public realm in order to contribute their bit to the restoration of the Atlantic bond, following in the footsteps of the brilliant pioneers of the 1950s and 1960s.

For Europeans, what is at stake is nothing less than the definition of a new Atlanticism. From the start of the unification of Europe and of NATO more than fifty years ago, Atlanticism and European activism have always been at odds. Concerned above all to maintain strong ties with the United States, Atlanticist governments and political parties have more or less vigorously obstructed any advance in European diplomatic and strategic integration. Conversely, the supporters of a "European Europe" and of a defense capacity independent of NATO, as advocated by de Gaulle, have made rivalry with the United States the principal axis of their political vision. These two antagonistic perspectives continue to dominate and to sterilize both the European debate and transatlantic relations.

The Europeans' inability to take charge of their own defense is thus still attributed to some mysterious American conspiracy. This was recently the case with respect to the proposed NATO response force, accused of being designed to torpedo the similar force programmed by the European Union in 1999, which does not seem about to come into existence. And the argument is made even though Europeans frequently complain that America is disengaging from NATO.

In a noteworthy article entitled "Clarifying the European Identity" the former French foreign minister Hubert Védrine illustrates the ambiguities of Europe's attitude toward its great historical ally.[10] The inventor of the "hyperpower" label for the United States writes:

> Perhaps it is time to recognize that Europe and America are cousins, but also that within this large community of values Europeans have their own conception of human and social relations and of openness to the world. It is also time to recognize that an affirmation of European identity would fit perfectly well in the framework of our friendship and our alliance with the United States. But Europe should behave as an emancipated, autonomous entity, as a partner, an ally for the United States, not a subordinate, provided Europeans want that result and give themselves the means to accomplish it.

This approach would hardly call for comment if it were not the immediate sequel of a simultaneous dismissal of Turkey and America from the "European identity" and of a rejection of any unifying concept—civilization or even area—whether "Euro-Atlantic," "Euro-American," or even "Western," all accused of blurring the identifying characteristics of Europeans and inhibiting their ability to project themselves in the world. Obviously, there is no question of making the European Union subordinate to the United States nor even of organizing what corporate executives call, often hypocritically, a "merger of equals." But the rejection of a privileged bond between the two sides of the Atlantic and the assertion of equivalence between America and the eastern periphery of the enlarged European Union say a good deal about the ambivalence of some Europeans on this essential question.

The recent transformations of the international system have nevertheless made the historical antagonism between Atlanticism and "Europeanism" largely obsolete and counterproductive. The time has now come to go beyond that antagonism by simultaneously strengthening transatlantic relations and building a European power on the international stage, for one is the indispensable condition for the other. The complementarity between a stronger Europe and a more open America and the prospects that their renewed alliance would open for the world militate strongly in favor of such a vision.

Europeans could help Americans share that conclusion by rejecting the choice between Europe as a power potentially antagonistic toward the United States and no Europe at all. In confronting the challenges of the new century Europe and America must more than ever stand and work together as the sentinels of liberty.

Notes

Preface

1. In this vein, see the Joint Declaration dated May 14, 2003, published by the Center for Strategic and International Studies, Washington, D.C., under the title "Renewing the Transatlantic Partnership," endorsed by a bipartisan group of former senior U.S. foreign policy and defense officials (www.csis.org), and a response by the board of directors of the new European think tank Notre Europe, dated May 29, 2003, entitled "Defining Together a New World Order" (www.notre-europe.asso.fr).

Preface to the French Edition

1. This line of thinking is illustrated by the book by the French sociologist Emmanuel Todd, *La Fin de l'Empire: Essai sur la décomposition du système américain* (Paris: Gallimard, 2002).

Chapter 1. The Empire on Trial

1. Jean-Marie Colombani, "Nous sommes tous américains," *Le Monde*, 13 September 2001.

2. Francis Fukuyama, *The End of History and the Last Man* (New York: Free Press, 1992).

3. As used in this book, the words *liberalism* and *neoliberalism* and the corresponding adjectives must be generally understood in their European sense, as referring to the market economy and political freedoms (as opposed to the American connotation of government intervention).

4. Jean-François Revel, *L'Obsession anti-américaine* (Paris: Plon, 2002); Philippe Roger, *L'Ennemi américain* (Paris: Seuil, 2002).

5. Each in its own way, Revel, *L'Obsession anti-américaine*, and Todd, *La Fin de l'Empire*, are eloquent on this point.

6. Earnings before interest, taxes, depreciation, and amortization.

7. Jean-François Richard, *High Noon: Twenty Global Problems, Twenty Years to Solve Them* (New York: Basic Books, 2002).

Chapter 2. Continental Drift

1. A good deal can be learned about this exceptional period from Pascaline Winand, *Eisenhower, Kennedy, and the United States of Europe* (New York: St. Martin's Press, 1993).

2. "Essai de définition de l'identité politique européenne," http://www.notre-europe.asso.fr.

3. On the contrast between demographic trends in Europe and the United States, see the special report "A Tale of Two Bellies," in the *Economist*, 24 August 2002.

4. See Denis Lacorne, *La Crise de l'identité américaine: Du melting pot au multiculturalisme* (Paris: Fayard, 1997).

5. See Simon Serfaty, *La France vue par les États-Unis: Réflexions sur la francophobie à Washington* (Paris: Centre français sur les États-Unis, Institut français des relations internationales [IFRI], November 2002).

6. On these questions, see in particular the note published by the Institut Montaigne, *La Sécurité extérieure de la France face aux nouveaux risques stratégiques* (Paris, May 2002); and Jolyon Howorth, "L'intégration européenne et la défense: L'ultime défi?" *Cahiers de Chaillot* 43 (November 2000), http://www.weu.int/institute/.

7. The new American strategic doctrine is set out in the White House document entitled *The National Security Strategy of the USA* (Washington, D.C., September 2002).

Chapter 3. The New Atlantic Imperative

1. Fukuyama, *End of History*.

2. Samuel Huntington, *The Clash of Civilizations and the Remaking of World Order* (New York: Simon & Schuster, 1996).

3. Francis Fukuyama, "Craquements dans le monde occidental," *Le Monde*, 16 August 2002.

4. "What We're Fighting For: A Letter from America," www.americanvalues.org. This document, published in February 2002 by the Institute for American Values, was signed by some sixty American academics

and other intellectuals of various disciplines, including Samuel Huntington, Francis Fukuyama, Michael Walzer, and Robert Putnam.

5. Francis Fukuyama, "Nous sommes toujours à la fin de l'histoire," *Le Monde*, 18 October 2001.

6. See, e.g., Antoine Babsous, *L'Islamisme, une révolution avortée?* (Paris: Hachette, 2000); and Gilles Kepel, *Jihad, expansion et déclin de l'islamisme* (Paris: Gallimard, 2000).

Chapter 4. Europe in Search of Political Will and Representation

1. See, e.g., the recent book by Charles A. Kupchan, *The End of the American Era: U.S. Foreign Policy and the Geopolitics of the Twenty-First Century* (New York: Knopf, 2002); and his article "The End of the West," *Atlantic Monthly*, November 2002.

2. The phrase "Community method" refers to the institutional model put in place at the foundation of the European Community, which ensured its success. It is based on the exclusive power of initiative of the European Commission, qualified majority voting at the Council of Ministers, and the supremacy of EEC law over national laws under the sole jurisdiction of the European Court of Justice. For further developments, see Laurent Cohen-Tanugi, *L'Europe en danger* (Paris: Fayard, 1992).

3. These are Poland, Hungary, the Czech Republic, Slovakia, Slovenia, the three Baltic republics, Cyprus, and Malta.

4. On this subject, see the incisive analysis by Jean-Louis Bourlanges, "La fin de l'Europe communautaire, critique du traité de Nice," *Commentaire* 95 (fall 2001).

5. Albert Cohen, *Belle du Seigneur* (Paris: Gallimard, 1968).

6. One among many illustrations of this line of thinking may be found in the speech on Europe delivered by the former French prime minister Lionel Jospin on 28 May 2001.

7. Robert Kagan, "Power and Weakness," *Policy Review*, June–July 2002, and the resulting book, *Of Paradise and Power: America and Europe in the New World Order* (New York: Knopf, 2003).

8. A more extended discussion of this issue may be found in Laurent Cohen-Tanugi, *Le Choix de l'Europe* (Paris: Fayard, 1995).

9. See Winand, *Eisenhower, Kennedy, and the United States of Europe.*

10. *Jacobellis v. Ohio*, 378 US 184, 197 (1964).

11. This concern is clearly expressed in a recent article by the former French foreign minister Hubert Védrine, "Europe: Avancer les yeux ouverts," *Le Monde*, 27 September 2002.

12. A useful discussion of these questions can be found in Jolyon Howorth, "The European Security Conundrum: Prospects for ESDP after September 11, 2001," *Notre Europe*, March 2002.

Chapter 5. America and the Challenge of a New Internationalism

1. Henry Kissinger, *Does America Need a Foreign Policy?* (New York: Simon & Schuster, 2001).

2. Raymond Aron, *République impériale: Les États-Unis dans le monde, 1945–1972* (Paris: Calmann-Lévy, 1973).

3. Joseph S. Nye Jr., *The Paradox of American Power* (New York: Oxford University Press, 2002).

4. On this subject, see the results of the worldwide survey published by the Pew Research Center for the People and the Press, Washington, D.C., in December 2002.

5. See, e.g., George W. Bush's speech at West Point in June 2002, his speech on Iraq to the U.N. General Assembly on 12 September 2002, and the White House document *The National Security Strategy of the USA* (Washington, D.C., September 2002). On the prospects for American foreign policy, see Julian Lindley-French "Les Termes de l'engagement, le paradoxe de la puissance américaine, et le dilemme transatlantique après le 11 septembre," and Pierre Hassner, "États-Unis: L'empire de la force ou la force de l'empire?" *Cahiers de Chaillot* 52 (May 2002) and 54 (September 2002), respectively, at http://www.weu.int/institute/.

6. Nye, *Paradox of American Power*, 143.

Chapter 6. For a New Alliance

1. See Todd, *La Fin de l'Empire*.

2. See Kupchan, *End of the American Era*.

3. See, e.g., the article by Zbigniew Brzezinski, "Comment l'Amérique doit vivre avec la nouvelle Europe?" *Commentaire* 91 (fall 2000), and my reply, "L'Europe et l'Amérique entre Brzezinski et Schröder," in ibid. 95 (fall 2001).

4. On this subject, see Laurent Cohen-Tanugi, "L'influence normative

de l'Union européenne: Une ambition entravée," in *Les Notes de l'IFRI* (Paris: IFRI, 2002).

5. For the results of this survey, see www.worldviews.org.

6. See Roger, *L'Ennemi américain.*

7. On this subject, see Pierre Lepetit and Laurent Viguier, *The United States and Climate Change* (Paris: Centre français sur les États-Unis, IFRI, July 2002).

8. For a thorough analysis of the United States' compliance with its international commitments, see the article by Professor Detlev F. Vagts, "The United States and Its Treaties: Observance and Breach," *American Journal of International Law* 95 (April 2001): 313–34.

9. Diana L. Ech, *A New Religious America* (San Francisco: Harper-Collins, 2002).

10. Hubert Védrine, "Clarifier l'identité européenne," *Le Monde*, 6 December 2002.

Index

ABM treaty, U.S. abrogation of, 43
Action Committee for the United
  States of Europe, 26–27
Afghan campaign, 16, 19
Albright, Madeleine, 119
American exceptionalism, 92, 101;
  costs of, 100–107. *See also* unilateralism, U.S.
Americanization of world, 2–3,
  117–18
Amsterdam treaty (1997), 66, 68
anti-Americanism, 1–20, 120; and
  George W. Bush, 17–19; during
  and after Cold War, 7–9; in European identity, 15, 34; globalization
  and, 5, 9–14; in reaction to September 11, xix, 1–2, 4, 14–17; traditional European, 4–5, 24, 120;
  U.S. foreign policy and, 5–9, 24,
  95; worldwide, 3–6
antipersonnel mine treaty, 122
Aron, Raymond, 91
arrogance, in U.S. attitudes toward
  world, 108–9
Asia, modernization in, 48–49
"asymmetrical threat," 99
Atlantic Alliance: areas of conflict in,
  21–25, 119–25; areas of convergence in, 117–19; after Cold War,
  xii, 24–25, 32–39; in Cold War,
  xvii–xviii, 25–32; European power
  and, 81–82, 114–16; European

unification and, 31–39; Europe's
  need for, 51–53; Europe's role in
  restoring, 59, 113–16; future sce-
  narios, 111–16; Iraq crisis and,
  xi–xv; need for, xiii–xv, 51–60;
  restoring, 59, 111–16, 126, 128;
  U.S. withdrawal from, 51, 53;
  U.S.'s need for, xiv–xv, 53–55;
  U.S.'s role in restoring, 59, 112–13
Atlantic divide, xi–xiii, xix–xxi,
  21–25, 29–45, 99, 111–12, 125–26;
  areas of conflict in, 21–25, 119–25;
  cultural (over "values"), 23, 36,
  116–17, 119–25; in defense capabilities and policy, 39–45, 78, 79;
  demographic, 38–39; economic,
  36, 37–38; European unification
  and, 32–35; in late Cold War,
  29–32; political, 36–37; public
  opinion and, 116, 125; after September 11, 15–17, 50–51; two
  views of, 111–12
Atlanticism, 30, 113, 126, 128

Balkans wars, 41, 51, 70
Brzezinski, Zbigniew, 32
Bush, George W., scapegoating of,
  17–19
Bush administration: criticism of, 4,
  5–6, 17–19, 22–23, 118–19; defense spending, 41–42; multilater-
  alism/ internationalism in, 107,

Laurent Cohen-Tanugi was born in Tunis in 1957 and educated in France and in the United States. A member of the Paris and New York bars, he has been a partner of the international law firm Cleary, Gottlieb, Steen & Hamilton since 1991, specializing in international corporate transactions and international arbitration.

Mr. Cohen-Tanugi is an alumnus of France's prestigious Ecole normale supérieure and holds an *agrégation* in French literature from the University of Paris, as well as graduate degrees from the Institute of Political Studies of Paris and the Harvard Law School.

He is the author of several influential books, including *Le Droit sans L'Etat: Sur la démocratie en France et en Amérique* (Paris: Presses Universitaires de France, 1985), a comparative essay on the French and American legal and political traditions, with a preface by Professor Stanley Hoffmann of Harvard University; *La Métamorphose de la démocratie* (Paris: Odile Jacob, 1989); *L'Europe en danger* (Paris: Fayard, 1992) and *Le Choix de l'Europe* (Paris: Fayard, 1995), both dealing with the political aspects of European unification; and *Le Nouvel Ordre numérique* (Paris: Odile Jacob, 1999), on the digital economy. A regular columnist for the French newspapers *Le Monde* and *Les Echos*, he lectures on these subjects internationally.

Mr. Cohen-Tanugi sat on the Commission for Judicial Reform instituted by **President Chirac in 1997 and is a frequent consultant to the French government and European institutions. A founding member of Notre Europe, a think tank chaired by Jacques Delors, he is an active advocate of European unity.

Mr. Cohen-Tanugi is a member of the French Academy of Technologies and sits on the boards of directors or advisers of several nonprofit institutions, including the Aspen Institute France and the European Law Research Center of the Harvard Law School.